THE BROOKLYN BRIDGE

They Said It Couldn't Be Built

THEY SAID
THE
IT COULDN'T
BROOKLYN
BE BUILT
BRIDGE

by Judith St. George

ILLUSTRATED WITH PHOTOGRAPHS

HARCOURT BRACE & COMPANY
Orlando Atlanta Austin Boston San Francisco Chicago Dallas New York
Toronto London

This edition is published by special arrangement
with G. P. Putnam's Sons, a division of The
Putnam Publishing Group.
Grateful acknowledgment is made to G. P.
Putnam's Sons, a division of The Putnam
Publishing Group for permission to reprint The
Brooklyn Bridge: They Said It Couldn't Be
Built *by Judith St. George. Copyright © 1982 by*
Judith St. George.
Printed in the United States of America
ISBN 0-15-304613-9
4 5 6 7 8 9 10   059   96   95   94

To David,
with thanks and love

· ACKNOWLEDGMENTS ·

There are two main repositories for the Roebling letters, notebooks, reports, cashbooks, blueprints, plans, drawings, photographs, scrapbooks and private notes. These are in the Roebling Collections in Folsom Library, Rensselaer Polytechnic Institute, Troy, New York, and in the Special Collections of the Archibald Alexander Library, Rutgers University, New Brunswick, New Jersey. I would like to thank the staffs of these two fine libraries for the assistance they gave me during the research and writing of this book.

I would also like to thank Blair Birdsall of Steinman, Boynton, Gronquist & Birdsall, Consulting Engineers, for reading and commenting on the manuscript.

THE BROOKLYN BRIDGE

They Said It Couldn't Be Built

Stranded Fulton ferryboats (in background) can't navigate the frozen East River.

O·N·E

IT WAS RIDICULOUS that the short ferry ride from New York to Brooklyn, which usually took only ten minutes, should take so long. Why, they had already been underway more than an hour. John Roebling, who definitely wasn't a man to be kept waiting, stood on the deck of the Fulton ferry with his fifteen-year-old son Washington and glowered out at the gray East River choked with ice. Beneath their feet the deck trembled under the added steam pressure needed to keep the big paddlewheels turning.

What this river needed was a bridge. Here it was 1852 and the only way to get to New York and the rest of the world from Brooklyn was still by boat across this treacherous East River. With a bridge it wouldn't matter if there were ice or fog or storms or heavy tides. Yes, the East River needed a bridge, and if there was anyone in the country who knew about building bridges, it was John Roebling.

John Augustus Roebling, trained in Germany's finest engineering school, had arrived in America in 1831 at the age of twenty-five. Since then he had not only become the first manufacturer of iron wire rope in the country but a builder of suspension aqueducts and suspension bridges as well. A suspension bridge is basically a bridge suspended by cables hung over towers and fastened at either end. Right now John Roebling was building a suspension bridge over the Niagara gorge that was the first suspension bridge in the world designed to carry railroad trains. Now, as John Roebling impatiently paced the deck of the ferry, he saw no reason at all why the East River shouldn't have its suspension bridge, too.

It was no secret that the people of Brooklyn had always wanted a bridge. New Yorkers, of course, didn't care one way or the other about a bridge. What New Yorker wanted to go to Brooklyn, for pity's sake? But it was different in Brooklyn. With no electricity or telephones, the only way the people of Brooklyn had of reaching New York—or even communicating with New York—was by boat. But it didn't matter whether the citizens of Brooklyn wanted a bridge or not. There were just too many problems. It would have to be long enough to span the nearly 2500 feet from shore to shore and high enough for ships to sail under it. It would have to survive the terrible East River winds, while its base would have to withstand powerful currents, eddies and seven-and-a-half-foot ocean tides. So, much as Brooklyn wanted a bridge, everyone shook his head and said, "A bridge is impractical and impossible. It cannot be done."

But the word *impossible* had never stopped John Roebling. In 1857, five years after that long, cold ferry ride from New York to Brooklyn, he submitted plans for a suspension bridge over the East River, which Horace Greeley published in his newspaper, the New York *Tribune*. At first people were excited at the possibility, but then wiser heads prevailed. "It's a wonderful dream, but who can cross a river on a dream? There are too many problems to overcome. No, it cannot be done."

The people of Brooklyn didn't know John Roebling very well. Though he was willing to put his plans aside for the time being, he didn't forget them. He waited nine years, and then in 1866 again proposed a suspension bridge over the East River. A lot had happened during those years. The bloody Civil War had been fought and was now over. Times had changed. The heroes of

John A. Roebling, the creative genius behind the building of the Brooklyn Bridge.

the new age were no longer the destroyers but the builders, and America's true destiny had become the mastery of nature.

The Roebling family had changed, too. Washington, who was the oldest of John Roebling's seven living children, had grown up, become a Union officer, served in the war and married. John Roebling himself had become famous. He had finished the Niagara Gorge Bridge, built the Allegheny suspension bridge in Pittsburgh and, in Cincinnati, was just now finishing the longest suspension bridge ever built. He was, in fact, the leading builder of suspension bridges in the world.

Despite John Roebling's fame, his second proposal for a bridge might have gone the way of his first if it hadn't been for the weather. The winter of 1866/1867 was one of the coldest, hardest winters ever recorded in New York. The East River, which really wasn't a river at all but a saltwater strait, was choked with ice for days at a time. Ferries were endlessly delayed or didn't run at all.

Now the people of Brooklyn clamored for a bridge. Newspapers took up the cry. Politicians joined the crusade. At last, on April 16, 1867, the New York legislature passed a bill creating a private company to raise money to construct an East River bridge. It was "An Act to incorporate the New York Bridge Company, for the purpose of constructing and maintaining a bridge over the East River, between the cities of New York and Brooklyn."

John Roebling's persistence had paid off. Fifteen years after he had first envisioned it, his dream of a bridge was at last on its way to becoming a reality.

Washington A. Roebling, age 19, as a student at Rensselaer Polytechnic Institute.

T·W·O

WHAT WAS THE BRIDGE to be named? John Roebling called it the East River Bridge, but at one time or another it was known as the Brooklyn Bridge, the Empire Bridge, the Great Bridge, the New York and Brooklyn Bridge and even the Roebling Bridge. John Roebling didn't care what it was called just as long as he could begin work on it.

It was as if John Roebling were in a race against time. He completed plans for the bridge only three months after the New York Bridge Company had named him chief engineer at a salary of $8,000 a year. When newspapers published his plans, people were stunned, not only by the size of the bridge itself but by its price tag—$7,000,000.

John Roebling's bridge was to be the longest suspension bridge in the world by half again as much. It was to cross the East River in one arching span, with its roadway suspended by four huge cables hung in catenary curves from supporting saddles on the tops of two granite towers. A catenary curve is the natural curve that is formed when a cable or rope is suspended from two fixed points, just the way a clothes line held at either end hangs in a

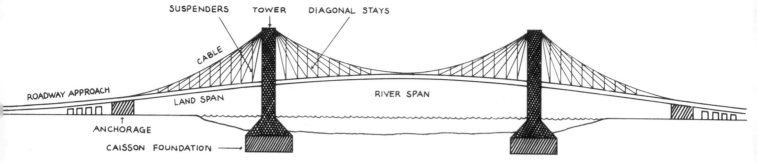

SUSPENDERS   TOWER   DIAGONAL STAYS

CABLE

ROADWAY APPROACH   RIVER SPAN

LAND SPAN

ANCHORAGE

CAISSON FOUNDATION

Diagram of a suspension bridge.

catenary curve. Two city-block-size piles of stone called anchorages, one in Brooklyn and one in New York, would hold the ends of the cables secure.

The river span, which was the suspended part of the bridge from tower to tower over the river, was to be 1595½ feet long. The land spans, which were those suspended parts of the bridge from each tower out to each anchorage, partly over land and partly over water, were each to be 930 feet long. Combined with the two roadway approaches, those sections of the bridge that started at the ground-level Terminal buildings and ended at the anchorages, the bridge's total length would be over a mile.

The two 276½-foot towers would rise from the river, one about 400 feet from the New York shoreline and the other off the Brooklyn shoreline, with bridge traffic passing through two tall, pointed arches in either tower. "The impression of the whole will be that of massiveness and strength," John Roebling declared. Massiveness and strength were hardly the words. The towers would loom higher and larger than anything on the New York skyline except for the slender spire of Trinity Church.

John Roebling was such an exacting and hardworking man that his son Washington once wrote, "The leading feature of my father's character was his intense activity and self-reliance. I cannot recall the moment when I saw him idle. . . . He never took a rest or vacation." Luckily Roebling had an artistic side as well. As a student, he had drawn beautiful freehand sketches, and before his left hand had been mangled in a piece of machinery, he had played the flute and the piano.

Now he designed the arches in the towers with an artist's touch. They were 117 feet high, far higher than could possibly be needed for traffic. Because of their graceful height and special grandeur, they would become more than just passageways. They would make the simple crossing of the bridge an event.

And with his artist's touch John Roebling designed a wide boardwalk for pedestrians, not beside the roadway traffic as on other bridges but well above it. The raised boardwalk would make the Brooklyn Bridge unique among bridges forever. "This part I call the *elevated promenade,* because its principal use will be to allow people of leisure and old and young invalids, to promenade over the bridge on fine days, in order to enjoy the beautiful views. I need not state that in a crowded commercial city, such a promenade will be of incalculable value," he said.

He designed the 85-foot-wide roadway for the traffic of daily life. The two outer double roadways were for horse-drawn vehicles, and the two center roadways were for cable-railway traffic. The raised promenade he designed for the human spirit.

Promenades were fine, said the experts as they studied the plans, but this bridge, which would weigh almost 15,000 tons, looked as frail as the spiderweb it resembled. Why, this bridge would thrash and twist and break right up as soon as the East River winds blew or heavy traffic passed over it. And Roebling planned to use steel in the bridge. Steel! Ridiculous. There wasn't a building in the country made of steel.

Everyone attacked the plans—engineers, newspapers, the public. All sorts of arguments were raised against it. But none of the outcry mattered to John Roebling. For him the bridge already had a life of its own. It had compelled him all these years as nothing else had ever compelled him, and criticism wasn't about to stop him now. He called in engineering experts, showed them his plans and answered their questions.

They were soon convinced. After two months' study the experts announced, "That structure, when erected according to the plans and specifications proposed by Mr. Roebling, will possess a strength of parts not less than six times the strain to which they will be subjected." In other words the experts gave the bridge their complete approval. The army engineers gave their approval, too, after recommending that the river span be raised an additional 5 feet to a total of 135 feet in order that ships might pass under it more easily.

THE ROEBLING PLANS FULLY ENDORSED, headlined a Brooklyn newspaper on June 25, 1869. Never one to waste time, John Roebling, with his son Washington, who was now a civil engineer like himself, was on the very edge of the Brooklyn ferry slip to look over the site for the Brooklyn tower not three days later. In order to see better the two men climbed to the top of a rack

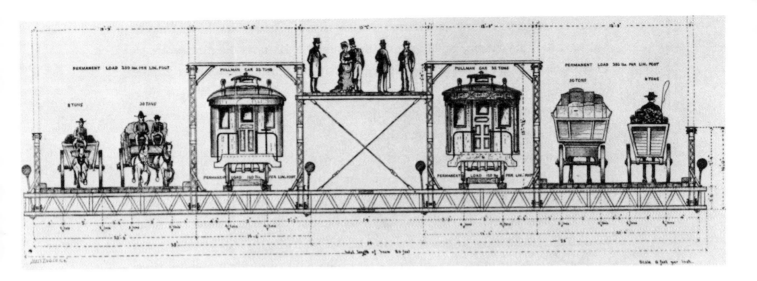

Cross section of the Brooklyn Bridge roadways.

of timber pilings. A ferry approached the slip coming from New York. Washington called a warning to his father, but the Old Man, as his mill workers called him, stepped only partway down. The ferry whistle blew again as the pilot reversed the engine to slow his speed. As the ferry slammed hard into the piling fender, John Roebling's right foot was caught between two timbers. The ends of his toes were crushed instantly.

Washington rushed his father to his own home in nearby Brooklyn Heights. The surgeon he sent for immediately amputated the toes and dressed the wound. But when he came back the next day to check on his patient, John Roebling made it perfectly clear that he was in charge now, and he would take no further orders from the doctor.

For as long as anyone could remember, John Roebling had believed that cold-water baths and soakings with cold, wet towels would cure anything. Now he ordered a special dish made that would provide constant running water for his foot. The doctor objected. It didn't matter. That was the way John Roebling had always treated illness and injuries, and that was what he would do now. As a matter of fact, he didn't care to see the doctor again.

As the days passed, John Roebling talked of nothing but the bridge and how he must get back to it. He became more and more impatient and difficult. Then he became more than impatient; he became a very sick man. Lockjaw had set in. Tetanus. When John Roebling could no longer speak, he wrote notes: notes about the bridge, notes about his treatment, notes about his finances. Then he was no longer able to do even that.

The Man of Iron died on July 22, 1869, at the age of sixty-three. John Roebling's dream of a bridge, begun on a Fulton ferry, would one day do away with the Fulton ferry forever. That a bridge demands a life is an old superstition that goes back to ancient times. How ironic that John Roebling's life should not only have been the first one taken, but that it should have been taken by a Fulton ferry as well.

T·H·R·E·E

NOW WHAT? John Roebling was the Brooklyn Bridge, and the Brooklyn Bridge was John Roebling. Was his death the death of the bridge as well? Not at all. John Roebling's vision lived on in the plans he had left behind. The only decision to make was who would be chief engineer to carry them out. That wasn't a difficult decision, either. A month after John Roebling's death, his thirty-two-year-old son, Washington Augustus, was appointed to the job.

Washington was a civil engineer who had not only seen action during the Civil War but had also built temporary suspension bridges for the army. He had risen from private to colonel in four years, been cited for gallantry three times and was known for his coolness under pressure. Forever after known as Colonel Roebling, Washington had not only worked closely with his father on two suspension bridges, but he had assisted him on the Brooklyn Bridge from the very beginning as well.

Father and son were very different. John Roebling had been a perfectionist, short-tempered, formal and not terribly interested in people. Washington was far more relaxed. He was better at working with people, more even-tempered, lighthearted and kindly. Although he was quick and bright, neither he nor anyone else considered him to be the creative genius his father had been.

Even their appearances were different. John Roebling was all bony thinness and harsh angles, with deep-set, penetrating blue eyes. Washington had a pleasanter, more open expression. His 1867 passport summed him up: "Stature 5 feet 9 inches; Forehead, broad; Eyes, light gray; Nose, short; Mouth, small; Chin, square; Hair, light; Complexion, fair."

Despite their differences father and son were both civil engineers, and as professionals, they shared important qualities of courage, determination, drive for perfection and complete confidence in their own ability. Faced now with the overwhelming task of building the Brooklyn Bridge, Colonel Roebling needed all the confidence he could muster. Luckily, as an officer, Colonel Roebling had worked and fought under pressure conditions during the war. Now he tackled the bridge the way a commanding officer would tackle a field assignment. It was as if he saw the bridge as a military adversary to be fought and conquered, an ongoing battle that he would wage on many fronts for a long time to come.

For now he had to order supplies and equipment, interview and hire assistants, get together a work force, evaluate manufacturers, attend to a hundred and one details. And just as he had had to give an accounting of his activities to his commanding officer in the army, so now he had to give an accounting of his every decision to the New York Bridge Company. From there his reports would be made public. He knew he would be held responsible for every step of the construction. He wrote later about that time in his life: "Here I was at the age of 32, suddenly put in charge of the most stupendous engineering structure of the age! The prop on which I had hitherto leaned had fallen; henceforth I must rely on myself."

Despite his doubts he took firm command. First of all, he knew the success or failure of the whole bridge depended on a solid underwater foundation. He had said earlier, ". . . upon the tower foundations rests the stability of the entire work." And Colonel Roebling had two underwater foundations to build, one for the tower on the Brooklyn side of the river and one for the tower on the New York side. He had already put a lot of time into studying how to do it. Two years before his father died, he and his young wife, Emily, had spent nine months abroad on an engineering trip learning about a recent European invention called pneumatic caissons, as well as studying new steel technology. After their stay in Europe, where their only child, John Augustus Roebling II, was born, Colonel Roebling made the decision to build his bridge on caisson foundations.

Constructing the first caisson, the one for the Brooklyn tower, turned out to be quite a job. The caisson was so enormous that it had to be built in a shipyard by a shipbuilder. The French word *caisson* means "coffer" or "locker," and that's basically what it was—an upside-down wood and iron box that was almost half an acre in size, 168 feet long, 102 feet wide, and 14½ feet high. It weighed 3000 tons and was constructed with an open bottom. The sides of the caisson were V-shaped, 9 feet wide at the roofline, tapering down to a bottom cutting edge of 8 inches that was shod with heavy iron. Five layers, or courses, of solid yellow pine each a foot square were laid on top of one another at right angles and bolted together to form the 5-foot-thick caisson roof. Later, once the caisson was located at its proper site in the river, ten more layers of timber would be added to the roof, for a total thickness of 15 feet.

To make the caisson airtight and protect it from sea worms, a sheet of iron extended over its whole outside. The inside of the caisson was coated with an airtight varnish, and all its seams were lined, or caulked, with oakum, like the seams in a ship. Oakum is simply loosely twisted fiber, usually hemp or jute, which is saturated with tar. For added strength 4-foot-thick walls divided the interior of the caisson into six work chambers, each 28 feet by 102 feet. Doors in these partitions were high and wide enough for a man and a wheelbarrow to pass through.

Meanwhile the site where the caisson was to be sunk was cleared and dredged. A rectangular basin was built to contain the caisson by driving three

The Brooklyn caisson in the shipyard before launching.

rows of piles deep into the riverbed, with the side toward the river left open.

On March 19, 1870, when the caisson was finally finished, it was launched in the East River with great fanfare, lots of speech-making, refreshments and a band playing. After all, this was the visible start of a great project, and three thousand people showed up to watch. But preparing the caisson site took longer than Colonel Roebling had expected, and it wasn't until May that six tugboats towed the caisson down the river. Colonel Roebling must have had mixed feelings as he rode down the East River on its long, flat roof. The caisson site was just off the Fulton ferry slip, where his father had been fatally injured less than a year before.

With only its timber roof above water, compressed air was pumped into the open-bottom caisson through two rubber hoses in its roof. It was like an upside-down rowboat floating in a pond. Air remained in the caisson, just as it does in an upside-down rowboat. It was here, in this airtight shell, that the men would dig down through the river bottom's silt and mud to reach a rock-hard footing. Once the caisson rested on a firm footing, it would be filled with concrete. The solid, concrete-filled caisson would then serve as the underwater foundation for the Brooklyn tower.

The East River would, of course, always be pushing to get into the working chambers. In order to keep out the water, as well as to provide air for the workers to breathe, six air compressors driven by steam and operating from the shore had to pump compressed air into the caisson day and night. Normal air pressure at sea level, or atmospheric pressure as it is called, is 14.7 pounds per square inch. That is, the air exerts 14.7 pounds of pressure on every square inch of matter. When the air is compressed, air pressure per square inch increases. As the caisson settled deeper and deeper into the river, higher and higher air pressure would be needed to counteract the increased push of the river. And the higher the air pressure had to go, the more difficult it would be for the men to function and work.

While the workers inside the caisson were digging down through the river bottom, men operating three derricks mounted on the caisson roof would be laying blocks of limestone for the Brooklyn tower. The 10-ton derricks had great wooden masts 55 feet high, like the masts of a ship, and booms that could swing anywhere on the deck. The weight of the stone being laid on the caisson roof, as well as the men inside digging ever downward, would sink the caisson deeper and deeper into the river.

These plans were all well and good in theory, but who wanted to be first down into this strange underwater monster? There was no need to ask. Colonel Roebling would be first, along with Colonel William Paine, one of his assistant engineers, and E. Frank Farrington, master mechanic. After all, the caisson was Colonel Roebling's special project and always had been. He was, in fact, the only caisson expert on the whole job. Furthermore, as commanding officer, he wouldn't ask his men to do anything more than he would do himself.

All was silence as the men gathered on the timber roof of the caisson just above the waterline. A workman pulled back the hatch cover. Colonel Roebling and his assistants stepped forward and climbed down the narrow ladder into the air lock. The air lock was a small, dimly lit room where air pressure could either be increased to equal the air pressure in the caisson or decreased to equal the atmospheric pressure at sea level. Before entering or leaving the caisson, the workers would have to pass through the air locks in order to adjust to differences in surface and caisson pressures.

Now the hatch clanged shut, and the three men were confined in the air lock. Unfortunately, the experience was something like being sealed in an iron coffin.

Sssssttt. Compressed air rushed into the air lock with the deafening screech of a steam whistle. The men clapped their hands over their ears at the sharp pain. They must have felt a moment of panic as their heads seemed almost ready to explode. Then, as the air pressure equalized, the terrible sound lessened and stopped. Now the air pressure in the air lock equaled the pressure in the caisson below. It was safe to go down.

First, always first, Colonel Roebling in his high rubber boots led the way down the ladder into the caisson. He held up his lantern. Eerie shadows danced on the wet, slimy walls. The compressed air had forced out all the water from the caisson, just as he had known it would. Still, it was one thing

Construction begins on the Brooklyn pier. Trinity Church spire can be seen in the background.

to see it on paper and another actually to stand on the muddy bottom of the East River. Astounding!

The work area was not only dark, but it was terribly hot and humid as well. The muck and water on the bottom were a foot deep in places. Colonel Roebling walked from one work chamber of the caisson to another. His voice sounded strangely faint. But he could breathe. He could move about. It would be possible to work down here. The caisson—*his* caisson—was a success.

F·O·U·R

THE BROOKLYN CAISSON was ready for the workmen. On May 21, 1870, 112 men, the first of three daily work shifts, descended twelve at a time through each of the two air locks. Most of the men were immigrants, Irish, German and Italian, and when skilled workers earned between $2.25 and $3.00 a day, these men earned $2.00, even for the night shift. It didn't seem like much, considering their working conditions.

Although the interior had plenty of headroom—$9\frac{1}{2}$ feet—the air was so saturated with moisture, the caisson always seemed to be shrouded in mist. It was dankly hot, too, and even though the men dressed only in trousers and boots, they sweated constantly. The compressed air made it hard to talk, and even the men's deep voices sounded squeaky. And to their surprise they found it impossible to whistle. Unfortunately, the flickering calcium lamps, gas burners and smoky sperm candles not only blackened the men's faces, but they didn't provide much light. After working a shift in the caisson, the men came out exhausted and irritable. Anyone who worked for any length of time in the caisson soon had a racking cough, and when cold weather set in,

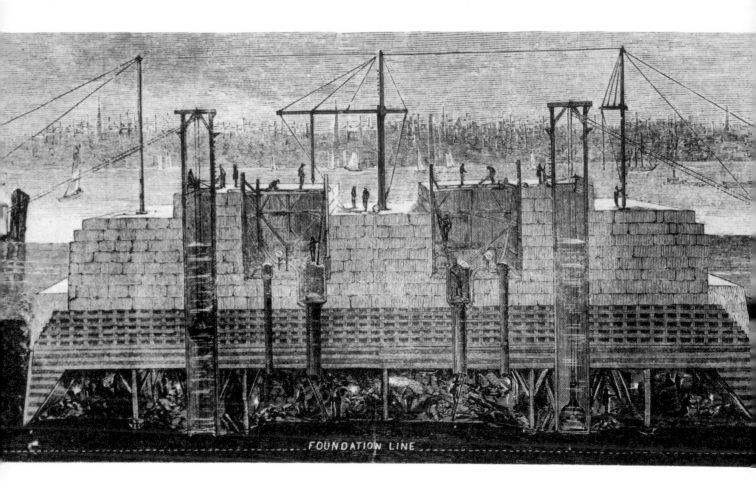

FOUNDATION LINE

Sectional view of the Brooklyn foundation, showing both the caisson below the water line and the tower rising above the water line. Workers descend through two center air locks into six work chambers. Supplies are sent down through the narrow supply shafts, while debris is removed through the two outer water shafts.

many of the men got bad colds and pneumonia. It was no wonder that one man out of three quit every week. In fact, the labor force on the job was so transient, a total of 2500 men worked on the Brooklyn caisson during the ten months it took to sink it.

Colonel Roebling's master mechanic, Frank Farrington, described the scene: "What with the flaming lights, the deep shadows, the confusing noise of hammers, drills and chains, the half naked forms flitting about . . . one might, if of a poetic temperament, get a realizing sense of Dante's Inferno!"

First the men had to shovel the gravel and clay and sand and rocks into wheelbarrows, then dump their loads into pools of water beneath one of two water shafts. Each of the big 7-foot-square water shafts, open at either end and built like a well, ran from the roof of the caisson down to pits that had been dug 20 inches below the working surface. Because the air in the caisson was under pressure, it was always trying to reach a less dense atmosphere. Therefore, in order to prevent the compressed air from escaping, the pits under the water shafts were filled with water and the ends of the shafts were submerged in them.

The shafts themselves were partly filled with water, with the air pressure inside the caisson holding the water at a fairly constant level. Every pound of pressure above normal in the caisson forced the water a little more than two feet higher in the shafts. The water shafts, therefore, were like barometers that measured the air pressure in the caisson.

Big dredge buckets operating from the caisson roof dropped down through the water in the water shafts and scooped up the mud and rocks that the workmen had dumped in the pools beneath the shafts. The rubble was then hauled up through the open-ended shafts to the surface, where barges waited to tow it away.

Even though his men worked hard, Colonel Roebling was unhappy with their first month's progress. Big rocks and boulders were more of a problem than he had expected. With no electrical power, the men had to break up the rocks with hand tools—picks and shovels and crowbars. It was an almost impossible task. The caisson was settling less than 6 inches a week,

The workers dump debris in pools of water under the square water shafts where it is removed from the work chambers by dredge buckets operating from above.

which meant it would take two years to dig down the 45 feet needed to reach a firm footing. That would never do.

Colonel Roebling knew he had to take drastic action, and now. He hadn't spent four years in the army for nothing. Explosives, that was the answer. Although explosives had never been used in a caisson before, no one had to tell Colonel Roebling about the dangers. He knew an explosion in the compressed air might rupture eardrums. Or damage air locks. Or result in suffocating smoke. Or worse, rapidly depress the level of the water under the water shafts, causing all the compressed air in the caisson to escape up the shafts. Without compressed air in the caisson, the river would rush in and flood everything. Or the 17,675-ton weight of the caisson structure itself might collapse and crush everyone and everything inside.

Risky or not, Colonel Roebling was determined to give it a try. As always, as chief engineer, he took the risk upon himself. He cleared the men from the working chambers.

Pooowww! Colonel Roebling fired a revolver with the smallest possible charge. It was all right. He suffered no harm, and neither did his caisson. He fired a larger charge. Still no harm. Then a larger one. And a larger. Now he was ready for the real test. He set off a small charge of blasting powder. The caisson was filled with acrid smoke and fumes, but that was the extent of the damage. He continued blasting, increasing the size of each charge until he finally set off an explosive that would be powerful enough to break up rocks and boulders. That did it. Colonel Roebling had found his answer. He had survived the explosions, and so had his caisson. Work could begin in earnest.

Work continued above the waterline, too. Block after block of limestone was being laid on the caisson roof. The stonework had begun while the roof was still above water, and now, as the caisson settled deeper and deeper into the East River, the limestone foundation of the Brooklyn tower continued to rise on the caisson roof, always keeping just above the waterline. It seemed as if Colonel Roebling were back on the battlefield, not only keeping action going on two fronts at once, one below water and one above, but also deploying his men and supplies, writing orders, keeping records, consulting with his aides.

Still, no matter how hard Colonel Roebling worked—and he worked harder than anyone—the campaign didn't always run smoothly. Soon after the caisson had been towed out into the East River, the first blowout had occurred. A blowout is what happens when that upside-down rowboat floating in the pond is tipped slightly or a wave changes the level of the water. A bubble of air escapes and rises to the surface. The same thing happened to the body of compressed air in the working chambers. Sometimes when the caisson pushed through the riverbed, it struck a soft muddy spot so it didn't settle evenly. Or at certain times there was a change in the tide. Or a passing steamer might cause a heavy wake. Any of these conditions could allow some of the compressed air to escape from under the edge of the caisson up to the surface. The bubble of compressed air would shoot a geyser of water, gravel, sand and even fish thirty to sixty feet into the air.

At the first blowout or two, the workmen inside the caisson were terrified. The thunderous roar, the sudden draft of air and the thick fog would have been frightening under the best of conditions, let alone working deep under the East River. After a while the men realized the loss of such a small amount of air wasn't a serious threat, and the noise and the minor inflow of river water were just another nuisance. Up above the workers were understandably frightened themselves when the first waterspout gushed up right beside them. But they soon got used to the blowouts, too, though the people who watched all the activity from the passing ferries never did get accustomed to the sudden geysers.

Certainly no one was prepared for "The Great Blowout." Early one Sunday morning a tremendous explosion resounded from the river. A waterspout that could be seen a mile away flew 500 feet in the air, splattering sand, mud and yellow water over ships in the river and houses in Brooklyn for blocks around. Witnesses said it looked as if a volcano had erupted, and the noise was so terrifying that people rushed from their homes and away from the river. Luckily it was Sunday, and no one was in the caisson at the time.

This interior of the Brooklyn caisson shows a worker descending a ladder out of the air lock.

Colonel Roebling, who was on the spot in minutes, described the scene. "The noise was so frightful that the whole neighborhood was stampeded and made a rush up Fulton Street." As soon as a good supply of compressed air had been pumped back into the empty caisson, he was the first one down. The descent was ". . . made with considerable misgivings," he admitted afterward. After all, he knew from the size of the blowout that all the compressed air must have escaped up the water shaft. Colonel Roebling was afraid he would find the working chambers crushed, or if not crushed, then no longer airtight.

To his immense relief, the blowout, which had been the result of a workman's failure to keep the water shaft immersed in its pool of water, had caused only minor damage. The caisson, which had sunk only 10 inches, was as airtight as ever. Colonel Roebling must have felt a sense of great satisfaction. And well he might. At the moment of the blowout, the caisson had been supporting a weight of 23 tons per square foot. When the bridge was finished, the caisson would only be supporting 5 tons of weight per square foot. Yes, between his father's original plans and his improvements, Colonel Roebling had built his caisson at least four times as strong as it needed to be.

F·I·V·E

AFTER THE GREAT BLOWOUT, work progressed on schedule. By December 1, 1870, the caisson had only three feet more to go before a solid footing was reached. To solve the problem of the caisson settling unevenly, blocks had been placed under the working-chamber partitions. As the caisson dropped, workmen knocked out alternate blocks, allowing the whole structure to settle evenly on the remaining blocks. Then the earth was leveled and the blocks that had been removed were again driven in. The process was repeated over and over as the caisson slowly descended.

The workers up above were on schedule, too. As they continued to build the limestone tower foundation on the caisson roof, they had been able to stay above the river at high tide. Colonel Roebling was well pleased. And then on a Thursday morning it happened.

Fire! Fire in the caisson!

It was the most dreaded cry of all. The compressed air in the caisson, heavily charged with oxygen, builds and feeds a fire quickly. There had been several minor fires before, all of which were easily put out. But this fire was

Fire in the caisson is a constant threat.

different. Though no smoke or flames could be seen, a workman's candle had ignited a fire in the oakum where the wood frame between two working chambers joined the roof. Because the compressed air fanned the fire outward, at first the only evidence of fire was a hole as big as a man's fist over where the candle had been set. It was evidence enough. The eighty men inside panicked for a moment. Then they got to work and turned the fire extinguishers on it. But it was useless. As soon as the carbonic-acid gas in the extinguishers was turned off, the fire flared right up again. It was a frightening way to learn that fire cannot be smothered in a compressed-air atmosphere. Try the water and steam hoses!

By the time Colonel Roebling arrived on the scene, everyone was exhausted, black from the smoke, but greatly relieved. They were sure the fire was out. Not Colonel Roebling. He knew that fire was his ultimate enemy. The fifteen courses of yellow pine wood in the caisson roof would last forever as long as they remained underwater and weren't exposed to air. But fire could silently eat through the timbers and destroy the entire roof so that the weight of the stonework overhead would come crashing through.

The general superintendent of work later said about Colonel Roebling, ". . . he remained in the caisson all night, putting forth almost superhuman efforts to extinguish the fire. . . ." First Colonel Roebling ordered water hosed on the timbers continuously. Then he instructed Frank Farrington to bore holes in the roof to make certain that no trace of fire was left. Colonel Roebling knew this was a risk itself. Compressed air would rush into every hole that was drilled. If even one ember smoldered, the force of the concentrated oxygen in the compressed air would act like a giant fan, flaring up the flames and sending them deeper into the timbers, where they couldn't be seen.

At last Colonel Roebling was satisfied the fire was out. He had spent all of Thursday in the caisson, and now, after working all night, he was so exhausted that he had to be helped up through the air lock. As he stepped out into the cold December air, he collapsed, unable to walk or even stand. Gradually he began to revive, so that by the time he arrived by carriage at his Brooklyn home on Hicks Street, he was beginning to feel better. It was time to rest and get his strength back. At least that was what his wife, Emily, wanted him to do.

But only three hours later a man rushed to their home with bad news. The fire had flared up again! Carpenters inside the caisson had been drilling holes in the roof to make sure the fire was out, and now they had discovered a mass of live coals in the fourth layer of the fifteen-layer timber roof.

Now the enemy and not Colonel Roebling was in charge, and that would never do. Weak as he was, he quickly dressed and headed for the caisson. But this time he only stayed down a few minutes. The fire had to be attacked aggressively, and aggressive action was what Colonel Roebling took. Clear the men out. Flood the caisson.

By now it was Friday morning, and it seemed as if all of Brooklyn had heard about the fire and come down to the waterfront to watch. Fire engines, fireboats and tugs were clanging and whistling and tooting their way to the scene. Thirty-eight streams of water were soon pouring down the water shafts into the caisson below. Within five hours well over a million gallons of water had replaced all the compressed air in the caisson. It was completely flooded. Now Colonel Roebling made another decision: Leave the water in the caisson over the weekend. Every square inch of timbers has to be soaked.

A writer of the time noted, "Caisson of the East River bridge was severely damaged by fire yesterday. I don't believe any man now living will cross that bridge."

Although Colonel Roebling may have had doubts, too, he never let on. On Monday morning he ordered that compressed air be pumped back into the caisson. Six hours later, as soon as the compressed air had forced all the water back up through the water shafts and the caisson was again filled with compressed air, Colonel Roebling was down inside. Every timber was dripping water, and except for one small opening where the fire had begun, he couldn't find anything to show there had even been a fire. What a relief. The concern had been terrible, but the enemy had been routed.

The next few weeks saw the caisson sink the final 3 feet to its permanent site at a depth of 44½ feet. Colonel Roebling knew once the men started filling the caisson with concrete, the equipment and supplies necessary for the

Colonel Washington A. Roebling.

job would greatly increase the weight load on the caisson roof. For extra support he ordered seventy-two brick piers constructed inside the working chambers. Once the piers were finished, the men could begin the concrete work. Because it was too cold to mix concrete outside, the men would have to mix the concrete inside the caisson, where the temperature always stayed at about 78 degrees. The cement, sand and gravel would be delivered to the working chambers just the way the quarter-million bricks for the piers would be delivered: through two supply shafts, iron tubes that were 45 feet long and 21 inches in diameter.

The workmen on the roof opened a locked door, dropped the supplies down the supply shaft, then relocked the door. Workers in the caisson below released compressed air from the working chambers into the supply shaft. As soon as the shaft was filled with compressed air, the workers opened the bottom shaft door, and the supplies would fall out. It seemed like a complicated procedure, but if the supply shaft wasn't filled with compressed air, the compressed air from the caisson would escape up through the shaft as soon as the bottom door was opened.

And that was exactly what happened just two weeks after the fire. Workmen on the roof dumped a load of supplies in the supply shaft, which got stuck partway down. Rather than clearing the first load from the shaft, the workmen above sent down a second load. The bottom door of the shaft fell open under the extra weight before the upper door had been closed or compressed air had been released into the shaft. Instantly there was a deafening roar as the compressed air rushed out of the working chamber into the supply shaft. The force of the air exploded stone and gravel out of the top of the shaft like shot from a giant shotgun. The men working on the caisson roof dove for cover.

Inside the caisson the noise was earsplitting. The lights blew out, and the air was instantly filled with a heavy mist. With the loss of air pressure, the water in the water shafts poured into the caisson.

"I happened to be in the caisson at the time," Colonel Roebling reported later to the New York Bridge Company.

The noise was so deafening that no voice could be heard. The setting free of watery vapor . . . extinguished the lights. No man knew where he was going; all ran against the pillars or posts, or fell over each other in the darkness. The water rose to our knees, and we supposed, of course, that the river had broken in. It was afterwards ascertained that this was due to the sudden discharge of the columns of water contained in the water shafts. I was in a remote part of the caisson at the time; half a minute elapsed before I realized what was occurring, and had groped my way to the supply shaft, where the air was blowing out.

It was a half-minute of wartime conditions. In the army Colonel Roebling had had a reputation not only for being cool but also for being on the spot when he was needed. He hadn't changed. With the help of several others, he closed the supply-shaft door so that the compressed air could no longer escape. Although that ended the emergency, everyone, including Colonel Roebling, agreed that it had been terrifying while it lasted.

Although Colonel Roebling lost no time getting his men back to work, up above, workers were noticing a strange turpentine smell coming from the caisson as well as frothy deposits in the surrounding water. Colonel Roebling feared a decomposition of wood was taking place. He tried not to show his alarm as he ordered Frank Farrington to drill two hundred holes in the caisson roof to check again on the fire damage. What Colonel Roebling found was even worse than he had suspected. The fire of two weeks ago had spread not only vertically through three or four layers of timber but sideways as well, sometimes destroying wood for a distance of fifty feet.

What should he do now? Because no caisson ever built was as large or as complex as *his* caisson, Colonel Roebling had only his own expertise on which to base his strategy. His decision was to fill the two hundred bore holes with concrete. He figured that the compressed air would rush into the holes, forcing the concrete up into all the charred areas, thereby reinforcing the timber.

Even after all the holes had been filled with concrete, at great cost and time, Colonel Roebling didn't trust his silent enemy. As a final check, he had a 6-foot hole cut in the roof where the fire had started. This time Colonel Roebling realized his enemy had almost won. His decision to fill the drill holes with concrete had been a terrible mistake. The timber beneath the concrete was covered with a layer of soft, brittle charcoal. It was like decay surrounding a filling in a tooth. And Colonel Roebling would permit no decay in the timbers that would support the full weight of his Brooklyn tower. His men would have to take out every bit of concrete and scrape away all the charcoal.

It was a terrible job. Eighteen carpenters worked day and night cutting away the burned wood and scraping out the concrete. Many of the timbers had to be replaced. Others were cemented. The whole job took more than two months and cost $15,000.

Although Colonel Roebling had finally defeated the fire, it had taken its toll in both time and money. More than that, everyone involved had paid a price, especially Colonel Roebling. Throughout the ten months it had taken to sink the caisson, the responsibility for every decision had been his, and though he had attacked and solved every crisis, he never regained his full strength from the night of the fire when he had collapsed. And he knew full well, even as the Brooklyn caisson was finally being filled with concrete in March, 1871, that he had a long, hard battle still ahead of him. Maybe it was just as well he didn't know how hard.

S · I · X

NOW IT WAS TIME to build and sink the caisson for the tower on the New York side of the river. Although it must have seemed at times that the Brooklyn caisson was going to bring Colonel Roebling to his knees, he wasn't about to let that happen with this second caisson. After all, Colonel Roebling was no longer a green and inexperienced recruit. By now he was battle-smart.

First he lined the entire caisson interior with a thin layer of iron boiler plate. No careless workman with a sputtering candle was going to start a fire this time around. For better visibility he installed double gas burners for lighting, ten in each of the six working chambers. Then he had all the walls whitewashed. Instead of the two old air locks that held only 12 men at a time, Colonel Roebling built two double air locks that would each hold 60 men. Now a full shift of 120 men could go down into the working chambers at once. Rather than six air compressors as before, thirteen air compressors would be going at all times. For added strength Colonel Roebling designed round water shafts instead of square ones.

Unlike the Brooklyn side of the East River, where the men had to dig through rocks and boulders, the New York side was mostly sand, quicksand and gravel. Colonel Roebling installed 58 sand pipes in the caisson to get rid of the debris. The narrow pipes extended down from the roof to just a foot or so short of the working surface. Workmen shoveled the sand and dirt around the open-ended bottom of the pipe. When the pipe was opened from the top, the compressed air rushed up the pipe, carrying the sand and gravel with it. Up above, the force of the compressed air shot the debris hundreds of feet into the air. Because the sand pipes were only 4 inches wide, the small amount of compressed air lost was insignificant.

Colonel Roebling designed the New York caisson with a 22-foot-thick roof, making it seven layers of timber stronger than the Brooklyn roof. After all, he knew he would have to dig down into the riverbed at least 78 feet before he reached a solid footing. That was 33 feet deeper than he had had to go with the Brooklyn caisson. Because of the caisson's greater depth, it would have to sustain 33 feet more tower and, therefore, a greater weight, on its roof. The New York tower would weigh 90,000 tons when it was finished, 20,000 tons more than the Brooklyn tower.

Even the shipbuilders had learned from experience. The building of the four-story-high caisson went as smoothly as even Colonel Roebling could have wished. Again, as with the Brooklyn caisson, the shipbuilders laid only five layers of timber on its roof, the other seventeen layers to be added when the caisson was in its prepared basin some 400 feet off the New York shore-line. Launching the caisson was such a gala affair that when six tugs towed it down the East River, Emily Roebling was among the party that rode on its roof.

Digging began in December, 1871, and right from the start Colonel Roebling was pleased. The new gaslights, combined with the whitewashed walls, made the working chamber as bright as day. Communication between the men inside the Brooklyn caisson and the men on the surface had been a real problem. Now one of Colonel Roebling's assistant engineers devised a primitive telegraph system that worked well. There were no big boulders to blast out as before, so that even the workmen were in good spirits. That is,

The sinking of the New York caisson.

they were until they found themselves digging down through what had once been New York City's main dump. Although the sense of smell is almost completely lost in a compressed-air atmosphere, the fumes from the sewage, animal remains and garbage were so bad that some of the workers were overcome. Because the black muck smelled only when it was exposed to the air of the caisson, the men had to keep the working surface under several inches of water as they dug.

Fortunately the sewage was only a few feet deep, and the men soon reached clean sand and gravel. Now their work really speeded up. The caisson was sometimes dropping as much as 10 or 11 inches a day. In fact, the men who were laying limestone on the caisson roof had to work fast just to keep above the high-water line of the river.

On the other shore the workers had finished laying the limestone for the Brooklyn foundation and had started laying the granite blocks for the tower itself. All the stone under the water was limestone from New York State, while all the stone above the high-water line was granite from Maine. By December 18, 1871, the Brooklyn tower already stood 78 feet above high water.

This was more like it. Colonel Roebling was well satisfied and he had every right to be. So far, he'd had only one problem. The compressed air shot the sand and gravel out of the sand pipes with such force, it was a real danger to workmen above. Once a man passing in a rowboat had the end of his finger taken off by a pebble fired from a sand pipe, and another workman was shot through the arm by a large fragment. After experimenting with several solutions, Colonel Roebling finally set granite blocks right above the pipes. The sand hit the granite and was deflected off into scows for dumping.

"The downward movement of the caisson has been under perfect control throughout the whole of the sinking," Colonel Roebling declared. Nevertheless, pleased as he was at this point, he knew the battle still wasn't won. The farther the caisson dropped, the higher the air pressure had to go in order to counteract the increased pressure from the East River. One pound of pressure equals approximately 2 feet of tidewater, so for every 2 feet the caisson dropped, one pound had to be added to the air pressure. With every added pound of air pressure, there was a greater chance of caisson disease. When the Brooklyn caisson had reached its final resting place at 44½ feet below the high-water line, the air pressure was 21 pounds per square inch above the normal atmospheric pressure of 14.7 pounds, and the men had already begun to feel its unpleasant effects.

A good deal more is known now about caisson disease and the effect on the body of working in a compressed-air atmosphere than was known in Colonel Roebling's day. The normal air a person breathes is made up almost entirely of two gases: oxygen and nitrogen. In the lungs the oxygen enters the bloodstream, which then carries it around to the body tissues to produce energy. Nitrogen normally doesn't enter the bloodstream and is exhaled without change. However, under compression nitrogen *does* enter the bloodstream and is carried through the body. When a person returns to the surface too quickly after being in a compressed-air atmosphere, the nitrogen forms bubbles in the blood. These bubbles not only block the oxygen supply in the bloodstream, but they also expand in the tissue spaces such as muscles and joints, producing the painful symptoms of caisson disease: stomach cramps, vomiting, dizziness, double vision, leg pains, paralysis. The victim's body can be so twisted by excruciating pain that caisson disease is often called the bends.

Colonel Roebling knew more about caisson disease than he perhaps would have cared to. He himself had suffered an attack the night of the Brooklyn fire. What worried him now was that he knew he had to take the New York caisson down to at least 78 feet to reach a solid footing. In January, 1872, with the caisson down to 51 feet and the air pressure at 24 pounds above normal atmospheric pressure, the men were not only suffering from numbing exhaustion after leaving the caisson but experiencing other painful symptoms as well. Out in St. Louis another engineer, Captain James Eads, was building a bridge across the Mississippi River with caisson foundations. Although his caissons were only a third the size of Colonel Roebling's, they had to be sunk to a far greater depth. By the time both of Captain Eads's foundations were finished, thirteen of his men had died of caisson disease. Colonel Roebling was determined that that wasn't going to happen to *his* men.

First he shortened the workday from eight hours to seven, divided into two work shifts of three and a half hours each, separated by a two-hour rest period. Then in late January, 1872, he hired Dr. Andrew Smith to take care of his men full time. Dr. Smith gave the job his very best, but he never really analyzed what caused caisson disease or how to treat it.

Although other factors were important, such as length of time spent in the caisson, diet, general health and physical makeup, the basic cause of caisson disease was that, after leaving the work chambers, the men were decompressing in the air locks much too quickly. Decompression was the process whereby the air pressure in the air locks was gradually reduced to equal normal atmospheric pressure. In other words, decompressing was that period of physical adjustment in the air locks as the men moved from the compressed-air atmosphere of the work chambers back to normal surface conditions.

Unfortunately, at a depth of 65 feet, Dr. Smith recommended decompressing in the air lock for only five minutes before returning to the surface. Five minutes were as inadequate as the two or three minutes that were all that the men wanted to bother with. Today the length of time a person can work under pressure and the speed of decompression are strictly regulated by law. At a depth of 65 feet the men should have decompressed in three stages in the air locks for two hours after each three-and-a-half-hour shift. If a person slowly decompresses in stages, the nitrogen in the bloodstream escapes without forming any bubbles at all.

The bends always occurred after the men had left the work chambers and returned to normal atmospheric pressure. If only Dr. Smith had known, the treatment for men suffering the bends was right at hand. The doctor should have immediately returned the victim to the caisson, then decompressed him in slow stages in the air lock. By decompressing the victim gradually, the nitrogen bubbles that had already formed in the bloodstream would dissolve, giving instant relief. It was a treatment recommended by Dr. Smith at one point but never used.

As the caisson continued to descend, the men became increasingly alarmed. Although they were now only working two two-hour shifts a day, air pressure in the caisson was at 33 pounds per square inch, and every one of them was suffering. Even though wages were up to $2.76 for a four-hour day, the men struck briefly, but in vain, for $3.00. The workers' families and friends were alarmed, too. If the caisson disease was a puzzle to Dr. Smith, it was a frightening mystery to the public. And then on April 22, when the caisson was at a depth of 71 feet, the first man died of caisson disease. Newspapers raised an outcry that the New York Bridge Company was allowing men to die unnecessarily.

The New York caisson operation, which had begun so smoothly for Colonel Roebling, had turned into almost total warfare. He was constantly in and out of the caisson with his men, going up and down through the air locks more than anyone, working twelve to fourteen hours a day, six days a week, often racing back three or four times a day by ferry to his Brooklyn office.

"The period of time at the end of the sinking of the New York caisson was one of intense anxiety for Colonel Roebling," Emily Roebling said later. It was an understatement. Although Colonel Roebling was near collapse himself, he kept up his killing pace.

As if Colonel Roebling's concern with caisson disease weren't enough, he was now forced to make the most difficult decision of his career. He could either stop digging at 78½ feet and let the caisson rest on sand and gravel, or he could keep going until he hit level bedrock. To continue would have meant enormous expense as well as time lost blasting the bumpy rock ridge into an even surface. More than that, Colonel Roebling knew it would mean more lives lost to caisson disease. On the other hand, he also knew if the caisson, which was to serve as the tower foundation, wasn't stable, the tower could lean or slip, causing the entire bridge to fail.

And then more desperately ill men collapsed. A second man died. Whether those events had anything to do with Colonel Roebling's decision was never known, but in May, 1872, Colonel Roebling gave the order to stop digging and fill the caisson with concrete. He had spent weeks testing the river bottom, and now he decided to rest his foundation on this bed of compact sand and gravel. "It was good enough to found upon, or at any rate as good as any concrete that could be put in place of it," he declared. It was an agonizing decision and a courageous one. His whole reputation and the success of the bridge depended on his being right.

Very little is known about what happened next. Probably Colonel Roebling didn't want much known. After all, the New York caisson had suffered a lot of bad publicity already. Not only were the public and the newspapers complaining about the caisson deaths, but they had also been accusing the New York Bridge Company of fraud and mismanagement. Of course, as chief engineer, Colonel Roebling was only an employee of the New York Bridge Company. However, in the public eye his name was synonymous with the bridge and every aspect of its construction.

Whatever the reason for keeping it quiet, in late spring of 1872, when the New York caisson was finally being filled with concrete, Colonel Roebling collapsed at the site. With his whole body racked by the terrible pains of caisson disease, he was rushed across the river by ferry to his Hicks Street home. It was the same house in which his father had died less than three years before. That night, Colonel Roebling was in such agony that Emily expected him to die, too. But it was as if he wouldn't let the New York caisson defeat him physically any more than he had let the Brooklyn caisson defeat him professionally. Although he was close to death for several days, he would not give up. Gradually he gained his strength back. Then, to everyone's surprise, with his usual determination he returned to work a few days later.

But determination wasn't enough, and work on a steady basis was not to be. During the next couple of weeks, Colonel Roebling suffered one attack after another. By September, 1872, with the New York caisson finally finished and work on both the Brooklyn and New York towers going well, he was so sick he had to stay home two or three days a week. It was a well-guarded secret. Although he had been sick for over three months, the newspapers hadn't mentioned anything about his illness and were still reporting that he was on the job.

In November Colonel Roebling ordered work on the already 145-foot-high Brooklyn tower to be stopped because of the winter weather. In December he ordered work halted on the 60-foot-high New York tower as well. December was the beginning of a long, hard winter in more ways than one. It was in December that Colonel Roebling decided that he was no longer able to go to the work site again. And he never did.

The New York tower above the water line. The three steam-powered boom derricks lift the huge granite blocks.

S·E·V·E·N

NOW WHO WOULD TAKE OVER the bridge? It was the same question that was asked when John Roebling died. For sure, if the newspapers and the public didn't know that Colonel Roebling was a very sick man, his assistant engineers and the New York Bridge Company certainly did.

Although others may have asked the question, Colonel Roebling never did. As commanding officer, Colonel Roebling may have been wounded, but he certainly didn't consider himself to be out of the action. In December, 1872, Emily Roebling met with Henry Murphy, president of the New York Bridge Company Board of Directors. Her husband was determined to stay on as chief engineer of the bridge, she explained. He was ill now, but he would certainly be able to take charge when work started up again in the spring. That was all right with him, Murphy agreed, just so long as construction continued on schedule. Emily told him it would.

And back in his house on Hicks Street, Colonel Roebling was doing everything in his power, and then some, to make sure that it would. He had to. At this point he was sure he wouldn't live to see the bridge finished. Still, sick as he was, he refused to give up. During that difficult winter Colonel Roebling wrote out detailed longhand instructions for everything that had to be done on the bridge, complete with drawings and diagrams.

It was an enormous job for anyone, let alone someone as sick as Colonel Roebling. After the first few days the terrible cramps and dizziness and vomiting had ended, but now he had pains and numbness in his arms and legs. He was short-tempered, depressed and no longer able to carry on any kind of conversation, even with his assistants. Nevertheless, he continued to work on the final plans for the bridge. By the time spring came his eyesight was failing, and he knew it was time to retreat. He requested a leave of absence, and he and Emily sailed for Germany for a six-month rest.

As it turned out, the trip did little to help Colonel Roebling's recovery. When he and Emily returned in late 1873, they traveled almost immediately with their son John to the family home in Trenton, New Jersey. The visit turned out to be a long one. Colonel Roebling and his family lived in Trenton near the Roebling wire factory for the next three years. That meant that Colonel Roebling's assistant engineers were in charge back at the bridge site during the time both towers were being completed.

Fortunately, except for their massive size, construction of the two towers was relatively routine. There could be no choice as to their size. Although the towers were actually hollow and not solid masonry as they appeared, they *had* to be massive. They had to be strong enough to withstand the tremendous downward pressure of the four cables passing over their tops. And the towers had to be high enough to hold the bridge roadway well above the height of the sailing ships passing beneath it.

The huge granite blocks used in the towers, weighing from 1½ to 6 tons each, were delivered to the stone yard three miles below the bridge by schooner, then landed by scow at the towers. When work went well, the men operating the three derricks could set twenty blocks in an hour. But work didn't always go well. Laying such enormous masses of stone at such great heights was dangerous, and altogether ten men were killed in accidents during construction of the towers. Three men were crushed by falling derricks. Some fell to their deaths. The others were killed by falling tools and stones.

By now, of course, everyone knew that Colonel Roebling was not only living in Trenton, but that he was also a very sick man. So who was in charge? There was no question in the New York Bridge Company office. Colonel Roebling was. Although his able assistants supervised work on the site, they were all following Colonel Roebling's orders. Letters from his Trenton sickroom sixty miles away arrived daily.

Each tower took four years to build. As soon as the Brooklyn tower was finished in 1875 and the New York tower in 1876, everyone's energies were focused on the two great limestone piles faced with granite that were known as anchorages. Colonel Roebling said, "In all suspension bridges the masonry usually forms about one-half of the total work to be done." Certainly all the weight and solidity of the bridge were in the caisson foundations, the towers and the anchorages.

It was John Roebling, Colonel Roebling's father, who originated the system of anchorages in bridge building and to this day anchorages are an essential part of suspension bridges. Each of the anchorages for the Brooklyn Bridge was the size of a city block and extended from street level to a height of more than nine stories. The name anchorage pretty much described them. Their purpose was to anchor securely the ends of the four great cables, as well as to form part of the roadway approaches that led onto the suspended section of the bridge. Despite their appearance, the anchorages, like the towers, were not solid masonry. To save on material and labor, arched passageways ran through them lengthwise.

Because Colonel Roebling, more than anyone else, knew how important the anchorages were for a stable bridge, he spent months in his Trenton sickroom working on their design. "In the anchorage, we have only two factors to deal with," he said, "granite and gravity."

Four great iron anchor plates were embedded in granite at the bottom of each anchorage. Each anchor plate weighed 23 tons and resembled a giant, multiarmed starfish. Eighteen anchor bars that were each about 12 feet long

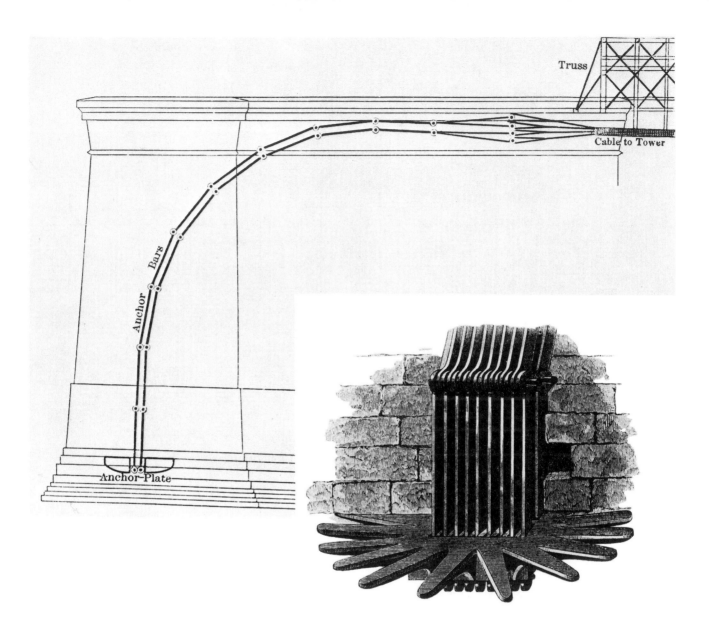

Truss

Cable to Tower

Anchor Bars

Anchor Plate

A cross section of an anchorage. Two rows of iron bars extend from the ground-level anchor plate (enlarged here) up through the anchorage where they are attached at the top to the cable strands.

and looked like huge dog-bone biscuits extended straight up from each of the four anchor plates in two rows. Eighteen more anchor bars were fastened by heavy pins to the original eighteen. Then another eighteen were fastened to these, and so on until ten links of anchor bars formed two 120-foot-long chains that curved gradually upward through the anchorage.

As each series of anchor bars was added onto the rigid chains, concrete and stone were built over them to hold them secure against the enormous strain of the cable strands that would eventually be attached to them. The last links in the chains were increased to thirty-eight anchor bars where they would be attached to the nineteen strands that made up each cable—two anchor bars to secure each strand. The last thirty-eight anchor bars, arranged in four rows, were left uncovered until the cable strands could be spun and fastened to them. These last uncovered rows of anchor bars looked like massive root systems sticking up out of the tops of the anchorages. Or perhaps they looked more like giant fingers poking up, ready to grasp the ends of the cables.

"All this is plain work," said a magazine of the day. And it was especially plain hard work for Colonel Roebling. Although the finished anchorages looked like nothing so much as two great stone fortresses, their planning and design were complex, and Colonel Roebling paid the price for the effort he put into perfecting them. His physical condition grew worse. Now talking with anyone but Emily was almost impossible. He was in pain a lot of the time and suffered from terrible headaches. He was weak and with such bad eyesight that he couldn't read or write or even sign his name. His nerves were shot. He was not, however, paralyzed, as gossip would have it. "This is a mistake as he has never been paralyzed for even one moment . . ." Emily Roebling noted later.

By now Emily was not only writing her husband's letters for him, but she was also reading aloud all written material that came to him concerning the bridge. Because Emily was the only person Colonel Roebling could talk to without becoming exhausted, he discussed in detail all sorts of technical bridge matters with her. Emily, in a real sense, had become her husband's indispensable aide-de-camp.

She came well prepared for the role. Her older brother had also been an engineer, as well as Colonel Roebling's commanding officer during the Civil War. The two men had been good friends, and it was through General Warren that Emily and Colonel Roebling had met.

Emily Warren Roebling was an attractive, popular, outgoing person, with such a good mind, she later graduated from law school at the age of fifty-five. She had even been able to charm John Roebling, her somber father-in-law. Colonel Roebling, with his usual humor, had described her in a letter to his sister during the war. "She is dark-brown eyed, slightly pugnosed lovely mouth & teeth, no dimples in her cheeks . . . the corners of her mouth supplying that, and a most entertaining talker, which is a mighty good thing you know, I myself being so stupid."

Living in seclusion with a sick husband certainly wouldn't have been Emily's role by choice, but she tackled her behind-the-lines duty with the same courage that Colonel Roebling showed in combating his illness. Just as he was determined to stay on as chief engineer, so Emily was determined to give him all the help he needed. And in the helping she soon felt as compelled and drawn to the bridge as ever her father-in-law or husband had been.

Emily Warren Roebling.

E·I·G·H·T

BY AUGUST, 1876, both towers and anchorages were basically
finished, and the first step in the cable spinning was about to begin.
Although Colonel Roebling was still in his Trenton sickroom and wasn't
there to watch, a great many other people were. Six thousand spectators came
to see the first steel working rope hauled across the East River.

One end of the rope was hoisted over the Brooklyn tower, then fastened
to the Brooklyn anchorage. The other end was wound on a giant reel aboard
a scow. As the scow was tugged across the river, the steel rope unwound from
the reel, immediately sinking to the bottom of the river. When the scow
reached the New York tower, the end of the rope was raised to the top of
the tower. As soon as the river was free of traffic, a hoisting machine on top
of the New York tower hauled the rope up from the bottom of the river. Up,
up went the rope until it was 200 feet above the water, plenty high enough
for masts to pass under it. Frank Farrington, who was on top of the New
York tower at the time, described the moment. ". . . The first rope swung
clear of the surface of the water, with a sparkling *swish,* amid the cheers of
many spectators and our own workmen."

The same day a second steel working rope was strung across the river the same way. The ends of the two ropes were then hauled down to the New York anchorage and joined, or spliced, to form one continuous loop more than a mile long that traveled from anchorage to anchorage over the tops of both towers. It was done! Brooklyn and New York were joined, and even if the joining was only by a working rope, the crowds loved it. "WEDDED— BROOKLYN AND NEW YORK UNITED" announced a Brooklyn newspaper.

Now it was time for a man to travel across the river on the working rope. More than a hundred people applied for the job, including a twelve-year-old boy and a professional acrobat. But Colonel Roebling from his Trenton post appointed a man who had worked with his father and him since the Niagara Bridge, a man, Colonel Roebling said, who ". . . has the necessary coolness and perseverance and does not easily get frightened in time of danger . . ."

The man was master mechanic Frank Farrington. And Farrington was anxious to do it. Like Colonel Roebling, he would never ask any more of his men than he was willing to risk himself, and the next step in the cable spinning involved working from this very rope while hanging 200 feet over the river. As Farrington said, ". . . on all previous works of this kind, I had found some difficulty in getting men to venture out to work on the ropes at first, and I thought my passage on the smallest of them would inspire confidence."

Once news of Farrington's ride hit the newspapers, word spread quickly. On August 25, 1876, spectators jammed both sides of the river, filling every available rooftop and crowding aboard so many boats and ferries that all traffic stopped. At least ten thousand people showed up to watch.

On top of the Brooklyn anchorage, Frank Farrington, dressed in a linen suit, climbed on the flimsy little boatswain's chair that was only 2 feet wide and looked like an everyday child's swing. Four ropes were drawn through the seat and fastened by a ring to the wire working rope over his head.

A huge American flag was unfurled from the Brooklyn tower and another from the New York tower. Since there were no telephones or walkie-talkies for communication, a man was stationed on the top of either tower with signal flags. The steam engine for running the rope started up. The red

Frank Farrington on his famous ride across the East River on the first working rope, August 25, 1876.

signal flag dropped. As Farrington sailed into the air on his way from the Brooklyn anchorage to the Brooklyn tower, the crowds in the streets below ran beneath him, shouting encouragement. Farrington stood up on the narrow seat, kissed his hand to the people and waved his felt hat. Then he was at the top of the Brooklyn tower. A great roar went up from the spectators, and a cannon on the New York side of the river boomed a salute.

Now it was time for Farrington's ride across the river. As he paused on top of the Brooklyn tower, he looked out. There was nothing to see but the wire that was to carry him across the East River disappearing into a gossamer spider's thread, with the distant granite-gray New York tower at the end of it. No one knew what Farrington's thoughts were, but he didn't hesitate as he climbed back on his narrow board seat. The boats that circled below in the water jockeying for a better position were suddenly still. The thousands of spectators on either shore were silent. The signal flag waved. The rope started moving. Now the crowds let out with a roar as Farrington sailed out 200 feet above the water. The wind blew his shaky perch so that it bobbed and swayed. There was no standing up this time, but Farrington did manage to wave his hat with one hand while he held on with the other. The boats in the river responded by blowing their whistles, tooting their horns and ringing their bells. The crowds cheered and shouted their approval.

And then, twenty-two minutes after it had begun, Farrington's breathtaking ride was over and he was on the New York anchorage. Church bells tolled, factory whistles shrieked and boats whistled. The only one who seemed calm was Farrington himself as thousands rushed toward the anchorage to lift him to their shoulders. He was an instant hero. As a magazine article stated at the time, ". . . his intended private trip for the encouragement of his men was a public triumph." But Farrington wasn't interested. With the crowds close to rioting, he hid in a nearby building. Finally he was able to make it back across the river by boat to Brooklyn.

The first man had crossed the East River on the bridge that could never be built. And in the crossing two great cities had been symbolically linked. It came at a perfect time. The year before the bridge, newly named the New

York and Brooklyn Bridge, had been taken out of private hands and turned over to New York and Brooklyn as a "public work, to be constructed by the two cities for the accommodation, convenience and safe travel of the inhabitants . . ." Brooklyn was to own and pay for two thirds of the bridge and New York City was to own and pay for one third. The New York Bridge Company was legally dissolved, although the same officers stayed on, now known as the board of trustees.

Now, after years of work, talk, problems, criticism, lack of funds, political feuds, and rumors of criminal corruption and mismanagement, the public was able to understand for the first time what this Roebling dream of a bridge was all about. Just a month after the nation's hundredth anniversary celebration of its independence, the bridge at last belonged to the people.

"I HAVE CARRIED OUT your instructions to the letter . . . I shall expect the cables of this bridge to equal, if they do not excel, the best that ever were made."

When Colonel Roebling in Trenton received this message from Frank Farrington, he decided it was time to return to Brooklyn. He was still sick, but it was as if the cables were pulling him back into the action. After all, cable spinning was what he knew and liked best. Since he wasn't up to traveling by train, he and Emily and their son John arrived in New York by boat. It was October, 1876. As the tug steamed up the East River, Colonel Roebling saw the bridge for the first time in almost three years. He had imagined it in his mind's eye for so long that the reality couldn't have been a surprise. Still, like anyone seeing it for the first time, he must have marveled at the sight of the huge towers that dominated the whole skyline. The working ropes stretched far above the river, ready for the cable spinning. Yes, it was time to return to the campaign.

The Roeblings moved into a new house in Brooklyn at 110 Columbia

"Pedestrians on the footpath of the Brooklyn Bridge—Women Faint in Mid-Air, while several men get sea-sick," wrote the *New York Illustrated Times*, August 18, 1877.

Heights that was perfect. It was about a half-mile from the bridge, and its rear windows overlooked the bridge from one end to the other, with nothing to block the view. Colonel Roebling, who was still too sick to leave his room, immediately posted himself by a window with a pair of field glasses. Like a wounded officer, he would direct the battle from behind the lines, with Emily as his aide-de-camp at the site.

Because no suspension bridge of this size had ever been built before, it had been impossible to find experienced workers. Hiring sailors and ship riggers was the answer, Colonel Roebling decided. They might not know anything about cable spinning, but Frank Farrington, who had worked on both the Niagara and the Cincinnati bridge cables, could teach them. At least as sailors, they were used to working at hair-raising heights while being underway at sea. As Frank Farrington told a reporter, "No sir, no man can be a bridgebuilder who must educate his nerves. . . . They must . . . be able to look sheer down hundreds of feet without a muscle trembling."

As soon as all the working cables were up, a catwalk or footbridge was hung from anchorage to anchorage over the tops of both towers. Through his field glasses Colonel Roebling could see the antlike figures making their way back and forth on the narrow footbridge that was called the "pathway to the sky." Most of the men didn't even bother to hold onto the handrails.

But Colonel Roebling noticed more than workmen in his field glasses. All of a sudden the footbridge became the greatest tourist attraction in town. People who had watched construction for seven years now saw the chance to be a part of history themselves. Hundreds applied for and were granted passes to cross the footbridge. But the average citizen wasn't a ship rigger by nature. The footbridge was only four feet wide, with spaces between the planks to lessen the wind factor. The little handrails were hip high, so that one wrong move would send a person right under them. Then there was that wind—that constant East River wind.

Some people got dizzy in the middle and had to be helped back. Others crawled to safety on their hands and knees. At least one fainted. Then there were those who thought it was great sport to jump and prance on the little bridge, making it dangerous for themselves and everyone else. Surprisingly, the tourists didn't seem to bother the workmen, and the sightseeing continued until the New York Bridge Company finally called a halt to it.

Now that the actual cable spinning was about to begin, Colonel Roebling made a major decision. He decided to use steel in the cable wires instead of iron. Although his father had considered using steel, calling it the metal of the future, it was Colonel Roebling who took the giant step forward. Steel was indeed the metal of the future. Iron wire was never used in suspension bridges again.

Colonel Roebling also took a big step forward when he decided to galvanize the wires by running them through a bath of molten zinc to protect them against rusting. One of the reasons the Brooklyn Bridge has resisted the elements for so many years is that Colonel Roebling not only galvanized the wires for the main cables, but galvanized all the steel wire rope suspenders and diagonal stays as well.

Colonel Roebling, still at his window post, couldn't see everything. For sure he couldn't distinguish the wires and ropes very well. But he had planned every step in such detail that he could tell by the way the figures were moving just what they were doing—and if they were doing it right. After all, Colonel Roebling had been in charge of all the cable spinning on the Cincinnati Bridge, and this cable spinning was the same, only on a much larger scale.

The galvanized steel wire, which was about 3/16 inch thick, was oiled twice, then rolled onto one of thirty-two drums set on top of the Brooklyn anchorage. Each of the 8-foot-diameter drums held nearly ten miles of wire that was carefully spliced to make one continuous length. The end of the wire was looped over a carrier wheel that looked like a big bicycle wheel suspended from the working rope. The loose end of the wire was then fastened at the rear of the anchorage to a 2-foot-long iron "shoe" that resembled a horseshoe magnet. When the steam engine started up, the working rope with the carrier wheel attached to it began its ten-minute journey from the Brooklyn anchorage to the top of the Brooklyn tower, and from there across the river to the top of the New York tower, and then down to the New York

The steel cable wire is spliced into ten-mile lengths and wound on huge drums for spinning.

A worker starts off the carrier wheel. Two wires are produced as the wheel crosses the river from anchorage to anchorage.

anchorage. Because the wire had been looped over the carrier wheel and then fastened, *two* wires were produced.

It is the same principle as someone holding a full spool of thread in his right hand and an empty spool in his left. First, he loops the thread from the full spool over the empty spool and holds both the end of the thread as well as the full spool secure in his right hand. Now, as he rolls out the empty spool in his left hand, *two* threads pay out, just as two wires were produced as one wire was unwound from the drum by the carrier wheel as it traveled across the river.

When the two wires reached the New York anchorage, they were taken off the carrier wheel and slipped over an iron shoe temporarily set back 11 feet from the front of the anchorage, just like the shoe on the Brooklyn anchorage. The carrier wheel was then returned empty to the Brooklyn anchorage on the working rope. Wire from the same drum was again looped over the carrier wheel, and as soon as the wire was fastened to the iron shoe at the rear of the anchorage, the carrier wheel started up again. As the working rope carried the wheel back across the river to the New York anchorage, two more wires were produced.

Two carrier wheels were crossing the river at all times. One wheel trailed two wires behind it from Brooklyn to New York on one leg of the working rope, while the second wheel returned empty from New York to Brooklyn on the other leg of the working rope. A cowbell attached to the wheels warned workmen along the route to watch out. As soon as the work was going smoothly, another set of carrier wheels was started up, so that wires for two cables were being spun at once.

"The network of wires across the East River is rapidly beginning to look something like a bridge," commented a local newspaper. Indeed it was. The giant spiderweb that John Roebling had envisioned on his ferry-boat ride twenty-five years before was finally being spun, steel threads in the sky, continuous and unbroken.

Next Colonel Roebling had platforms built along the route of the wires and at the same elevation. Each platform, or cradle as it was called, was 40 feet long and 4 feet wide. The cradles were hoisted in place by derricks mounted on the tops of the towers and placed in pairs across the spans, one pair of cradles between the Brooklyn anchorage and the Brooklyn tower, three pairs over the river between the Brooklyn tower and the New York tower and one pair between the New York tower and the New York anchorage.

These cradles, which looked like painters' scaffoldings and were reached by using the footbridge, had to be hung crosswise to the wires so the men stationed on them could reach all four sets of cable wires. The primary job of these men, who were called regulators, was to make sure that every wire lay perfectly parallel to one of four guide wires against which all the wires were adjusted. The regulators signaled with flags for the men on the anchorages and towers to lower or raise the wires as was necessary.

Since it was easier to lower a wire than raise it, all the wires were adjusted 60 feet above their eventual position. This added height also provided the extra tension which was needed to straighten out the wires. Although it was originally hoped that more than two circuits of wire could be spun at once, adjusting each set of wires took about half an hour, and the men found it impossible to handle more than two sets at a time.

The workers were also restricted by the weather. Ice or snow on the wires closed down work altogether. But the effects of wind, temperature and sun made adjusting the wires difficult, too. The length of wire expanded or contracted with changes in the temperature. Direct sunlight could expand one section of wire, while another section in the shadows might contract. Ideally, a windless, cloudy day was best for adjusting wires.

When the carrier wheel had spun 282 wires, the men on the cradles tied and bound the wires every 15 inches into a solid bundle about three inches thick that was called a strand. Because each strand had only two ends, these 282 wires were not separate wires, of course, but 185 miles of continuous wire. After the strand was bound, it had to be fastened permanently to the anchor bars in the anchorages. With a hoisting machine the bound strand, on its shoe, was eased off the temporary support at the rear of the anchorage and

The wooden footbridge extends from the Brooklyn anchorage to the New York anchorage. Here a pair of cradles is being attached from which workers can adjust the wires during spinning.

A cable strand breaks loose on the New York anchorage, killing two men and injuring two others.

attached to two of the thirty-eight anchor bars that extended out like giant fingers from the front end of the anchorage that faced the tower. Because there was a strain of 75 tons on each strand as it was shifted to the anchor bars, this operation was the most dangerous part of the cable spinning.

Each strand had to be lowered into permanent position on top of the towers, too. The strands, which were in no way fastened to the towers except by friction, rested on top of the towers in four big U-shaped brackets called saddles. The saddles, in turn, rested on rollers, which moved back and forth according to the pull of the cables. Once the bridge was completed, the saddles weren't expected to move, but for now, this ability to move would provide for the stretch of the cables when the roadway loads were hung on them.

Spinning the cables in the air from anchorage to anchorage, with each wire having the same sag and curve as every other wire, assured uniform tension. Each wire gave up its identity and combined its individual strength to make a single cable of unified strength. John Roebling had said, "All the wires being placed parallel to each other, uniformly strained throughout and not twisted, the greatest strength will be obtained by the least quantity of wire."

The wire-spinning machinery hummed along day after day, week after week. It was going better than Colonel Roebling or anyone else could have hoped for. With good weather the men were laying up fifty wires a day. On their best day they spun 88⅗ miles of wire. And then it happened. In June, 1878, Frank Farrington and four other men were on top of the New York anchorage, easing off a strand to attach it to the anchor bars, when there was an explosion like a shot out of a cannon. The steel rope that held the strand had snapped.

Swooosh! Released from enormous tension, the heavy strand flew across the anchorage like a giant whip, instantly killing one man, seriously injuring two others and sweeping a fourth 80 feet to the ground with fatal injuries. Only Frank Farrington was unhurt.

From the anchorage the strand sailed out 500 feet into the air, slicing a telegraph pole in two and shattering a chimney. It lay still for a moment in the bridge yard; then the weight of the strand from midstream sent it hurtling over the top of the New York tower and out into the river, where it just missed hitting a ferryboat full of passengers. As the strand smacked the water, a 50-foot spray soaked everyone on board. They were lucky only to get wet. The lethal strand had demolished everything in its path.

It's unlikely that Colonel Roebling saw the accident through his field glasses. But he certainly heard about it, and the news didn't come at a very good time. Just when work on the bridge was going more smoothly than it ever had, a sniping attack had opened fire from the rear. Two months earlier a man working on the roadway behind the Brooklyn anchorage had been killed in an accident that had raised questions about the quality of construction material. Now, with more deaths, the newspapers and public were enraged, demanding explanations. Then the questioning took a disagreeable turn. It focused on Colonel Roebling and his ability to continue as chief engineer.

T·E·N

THE CONTROVERSY THAT BOILED around Colonel Roebling was understandable. The strand breaking had frightened a lot of people. Was the equipment shoddy? Was it safe to work on the bridge? Where was Colonel Roebling? A giant of a bridge such as this needed a chief engineer on the job, not supervising from an upstairs window.

There had been rumors before. After all, it had been six years since Colonel Roebling had fallen sick, and hardly anyone had seen him since. But now the rumors intensified. Colonel Roebling was completely paralyzed, it was said. His wife had to feed him. His mind was gone. Even, it was reported, he was dead.

In some ways Colonel Roebling had only himself to blame. He allowed no one in his room except his assistant engineers and a few trusted members of the New York Bridge Company. And he, of course, never left home. Not only was Colonel Roebling isolated, but every letter, report or communication from him still arrived in Emily's handwriting. Colonel Roebling wasn't yet able to read or write, and as a matter of fact, it was true that he was barely able to feed himself. It was no wonder that everyone was whispering that Emily was the true chief engineer of the bridge.

Actually Emily Roebling *had* taken over many duties of the East River Bridge, as it was now being called. It would have been hard for her not to. After all, she had spent years reading aloud to her husband every detail concerning bridge business. Not only that, but Colonel Roebling had dictated all reports, letters, instructions and even his daily journal to her. They talked over bridge problems together. She met with the trustees of the New York Bridge Company as well as with contractors and businessmen to discuss supplies and orders and deadlines. She went to the work site almost every day, sometimes two or three times a day, to consult with the assistant engineers, to clarify instructions, to check on the work. With that kind of day-in and day-out exposure, and with her keen intelligence and special aptitude for math, Emily was bound to take on an important role in the running of the bridge.

Nevertheless, helpful as Emily was and capable as the assistant engineers were, it was still the invalided Colonel Roebling who was completely and totally in charge. His instructions, though in Emily's handwriting, were so technically detailed that only an engineer of Colonel Roebling's background and experience could have dictated them. Any changes from John Roebling's original plans—and there were many—were Colonel Roebling's changes. Any decisions to be made, no matter how minor, were Colonel Roebling's decisions. Of all the rumors that were circulating, the most ridiculous was that Colonel Roebling's mind was gone. His mind was as keen as, if not keener than, ever.

As it turned out, rumors weren't the only enemy Colonel Roebling had to fight. Now, in 1878, New York City refused to pay its one-third share of the bridge costs, as had been agreed when the bridge was turned over to the cities. New York claimed that because the bridge would be a hazard to shipping, commerce on the East River would be ruined. Months passed, and still New York refused to pay the $500,000 it currently owed. To continue work on the bridge was impossible. It was like trying to send an army into battle without

The Board of Trustees of the New York Bridge Company on the Brooklyn anchorage at
the point where the strands are attached to the anchor bars.

Work continues in all kinds of weather. Men riding in a buggy wrap the cable with soft iron wire.

proper equipment or supplies. There was nothing to do but shut down the whole operation except for the cable spinning. In August, 1878, six hundred men were let go. With jobs hard to find, it was a difficult period for them.

It was a difficult period for Colonel Roebling, too. Almost everyone connected with the bridge had at one time or another been accused of corruption, bribery, political scheming or some kind of scandal. Now it was the colonel's turn. The John A. Roebling's Sons factory in Trenton had produced the steel wire rope used in the bridge, and now critics were suggesting that the factory was involved in dishonest deals. Not only that, but Colonel Roebling's loyal assistant engineers were accused of taking bribes from steel manufacturers as well.

This enemy wasn't a physical enemy to confront and defeat like sinking the caissons or building the towers. This was guerrilla warfare, shadowy and hard to fight. The gossip and rumors continued. At last a committee was formed to investigate the charges. After a month's study the committee decided it was all a giant misunderstanding. Both the Roebling company and the assistant engineers were completely cleared. Cleared or not, Colonel Roebling never forgot the bitter experience.

Then, gradually, the situation began to improve. In May, 1879, the courts forced New York City to pay the $500,000 it owed. With Colonel Roebling still directing the action from his upstairs window, full-time work started up again.

Sixteen months after the spinning had begun, all the strands were at last fastened to the anchor bars in the anchorages and lowered into the saddles. To prevent rust and corrosion, the cable strands were attached to the anchor bars 25 feet inside the anchorages, in enclosed vaults that could be entered by manholes for future inspection. To protect the cable strands on top of the towers from the weather, stonework was built up 5 feet above the saddles, leaving them in a kind of pit. All in all, it had taken 23,000 trips over the river by the carrier wheels to finish the four cables, each of which consisted of approximately 3,600 miles of wire.

Now the strand bindings were removed, the strands squeezed together and the whole cable wrapped with soft iron wire. The men who squeezed, or compacted, the cables rode in buggies, 10-foot by 6-foot boxes suspended from overhead trolley wheels that ran along the bundled wires. The men in the buggies let themselves down from the towers by releasing a long rope. Three men working with one wrapping machine were able to wrap 20 feet of cable a day. Once the four cables were compacted and wrapped, they were painted white. The finished cables were each 15¾ inches in diameter and looked like giant steel pipes.

Five-inch-wide iron suspender bands, each weighing 65 pounds, were now fastened around the four cables at 7½-foot intervals from anchorage to anchorage. Steel wire ropes called suspenders were attached to these cable bands by sockets. Suspenders was a good name. The roadway would eventually be suspended by stirrup rods from these steel wire ropes. The shortest suspenders, which were less than 3 feet long and made of solid rods, were in the center of the river span, where the cables curved down to meet the roadway. The longest suspenders were closest to the towers and were 170 feet long. Each of the 1520 suspenders was capable of sustaining a weight of more than 50 tons.

As soon as all the suspenders had been hung in place, the steel floor beams for the roadway were attached to them. The men began by laying the floor beams through the arches in the two towers. From there they worked out over the water from both towers and anchorages. By December, 1880, the floor beams had been hung from tower to tower. The end was finally in sight. The skeleton of the span arched gracefully over the river, to be met in the center by the downward curve of the four cables.

Although John Roebling's original plans had called for iron in the trusses, Colonel Roebling now decided to use steel. The trusses were an open framework of vertical posts tied together with diagonal braces that ran along the entire length of the bridge. A good deal of the strength, rigidity and stability that characterized Roebling bridges were a result of the trusses. They served to stiffen the roadway, distribute the weight of the live load, or traffic load, along the length of the bridge, as well as steady the bridge against the powerful East River winds.

Wire rope suspenders, hung from the finished cables, support the bridge floor. Travelers aboard the Fulton ferries watch the construction with interest.

Floor beams being attached to the suspenders. Even this late in construction, the footbridge is still in use.

Now Colonel Roebling had one last battle to fight. In 1881 he decided to add an additional 1000 tons of steel to the trusses. Although the additional steel would make the roadway strong and rigid enough to carry the weight of railroad trains, it would mean extra expense and extra time as well.

There was an instant reaction. Eleven years had passed since the bridge was begun, and everyone was outraged at the possibility of another delay. The cost was already well above the original estimate. Not only that, but twenty lives had been lost so far. More than half of the board of trustees of the New York Bridge Company had never even met Colonel Roebling, and of course he hadn't set foot near the bridge in almost nine years. The same old questions were raised again, both by the public and in the offices of the New York Bridge Company. Does the chief engineer know what he is doing? Has he gone insane? The board of trustees asked Colonel Roebling to appear before them.

His reply? "I am not well enough to attend the meetings of the Board, as I can talk for only a few moments at a time, and cannot listen to conversation if it is continued very long . . . I did not telegraph you before the last meeting that I was sick and could not come, because everyone knows I am sick, and they must be as tired as I am of hearing my health discussed in the newspapers."

Upon receiving Colonel Roebling's refusal, some of the newer and younger members of the board suggested that Colonel Roebling resign. When Colonel Roebling heard that, he had one answer. Never! His father was dead. His own health was ruined. For years he and his wife had lived only for the bridge. The struggle was almost over.

All right, then, the board ruled, if you won't resign, then we'll take a vote to decide whether you'll stay on. The board was pretty much split. The old-timers who had been with Colonel Roebling and his father before him wanted him to continue. The younger members were determined to make sweeping reforms in a period that was experiencing all kinds of political and social reforms. They wanted Colonel Roebling out. Word of the conflict leaked, and newspapers and the public took sides, too. Colonel Roebling stayed out of it. His work had to speak for itself. Apparently his work did speak for itself, for after much arguing, the board voted 10 to 7 to keep him on as chief engineer. A MAJORITY FOR ROEBLING headlined the *New York Times* on September 12, 1882.

The extra steel was added to the trusses, and the roadway was completed. Three slip joints were built into the trusses and framework, one in the center of each of the three spans. As the steel, which extended out from the span ends, expanded in the hot weather and contracted in the cold, the slip joints, with a capability of moving 14 to 16 inches, provided needed flexibility. The main span was built to rise and fall vertically as well. Roebling genius had built into the bridge this ability to move and stay alive when traffic loads changed drastically or when extremes of temperature caused the steel to expand or contract. As a trustee of the New York Bridge Company said when the bridge was finished, "It [the bridge] looks like a motionless mass of masonry and metal; but as a matter of fact, it is instinct with motion. There is not a particle of matter in it which is at rest, even for the minutest portion of time."

And then the roadway was finished. Sweeping upward, the roadway was 15 feet higher at the center of the bridge than it was at the towers and 46 feet higher at the center than at the anchorages. All in all, the elevation of the roadway in the land spans increased 3¼ feet for every 100 feet of bridge.

Next the diagonal stays were hung in place. Diagonal stays were steel wire ropes running diagonally from the tops of both towers down to the river- and land-span roadways. Fanning out, the stays connected with every other suspender at the point where the suspender and the supporting beam of the roadway met. The first stay connected approximately 70 feet from the center of the tower with the last stay connecting approximately 430 feet from the tower. These 400 stays crossed the wire rope suspenders diagonally for extra strength and rigidity as well as to serve as wind braces. They were so strong, in fact, that John Roebling in his original plans had written, "The supporting power of the stays alone will be 15,000 tons, ample to hold up the floor. If the cables were removed, the bridge would sink in the center, but would not fall."

Workers clamp diagonal stays to the suspenders. Sailors and ship riggers were hired for much of the hazardous work.

But the stays provided more than strength. They provided beauty. The stays, angling across and clamped to the suspenders, were the finishing threads that completed the beautiful giant steel spiderweb stretching across the river.

In early May, 1883, the 15-foot-7-inch-wide boardwalk for pedestrians raised 11½ feet above the traffic roadway was finished, and the bridge was basically done. The dead load of the bridge, which was the weight of the bridge itself and included everything but the caisson foundations, towers and anchorages, weighed 14,680 tons.

At last the roadway approaches were finished, too. The roadway approaches were a series of brick arches laid on limestone foundations and faced with granite to match the towers and anchorages. The roadway approach onto the Brooklyn side of the bridge, starting at the ground-level terminal building and leading gradually up to the anchorage, was 971 feet long, while the New York approach, from ground-level terminal building to anchorage, was 1562½ feet long. Because so much of the 5989-foot-long bridge was over land, $3,800,000 had been spent to buy up the neighboring real estate. Not only was the cost high, but demolishing old buildings, clearing out the land and constructing nine different bridges over city streets in order to build the approaches had been an enormous job that had taken more than five years.

It was time for a formal crossing. Emily, the assistant engineers, the board of trustees and the mayors of both Brooklyn and New York had walked across informally on a footpath of planks before the roadway was completed. But now a carriage was to be driven across. Colonel Roebling asked that his wife again have the honor, and everyone agreed. Emily Warren Roebling, the "peacemaker," was beloved by all. She worked well with the assistant engineers, the manufacturers, the contractors, the workmen and even the often-difficult board of trustees. And she was still her husband's aide-de-camp in the strongest sense of the word.

A driver in a sharp new victoria carriage picked up Emily at her house and headed for the bridge. She carried with her a live rooster in a cage as a symbol of victory. As she drove across the bridge from one end to the other, every workman along her route cheered and raised his hat in a salute. The

Buildings being demolished in order to build the New York approach.

Archway under the New York approach.

victory salute wasn't just for Emily. It belonged to all three Roeblings—to John, whose genius had designed the historic bridge and who was dead all these years; to Emily, who had devoted her life to her husband and his work; but most of all to Colonel Washington A. Roebling, who had planned the campaign, joined the fray, been felled, then carried on from behind the lines until the victory was won.

Colonel Roebling in his upstairs room with the completed Brooklyn Bridge in view from his window.

E·L·E·V·E·N

WHAT A CELEBRATION the bridge opening turned out to be. Brooklyn had never seen anything like it and neither had New York. Brooklyn schools were closed. Businesses and shops shut down, too. May 24, 1883, was called the People's Day, and that was just what it was. Thousands and thousands of people came, by cart and farm wagon, by carriage, by stagecoach, by steamer and boat, by foot. The railroads put on special trains. The President of the United States, Chester A. Arthur, arrived by train and so did New York Governor Grover Cleveland. With every big hotel sold out, it didn't seem possible that one more person could cram into the city, but still they came.

The *New York Times* commented, "Colonel Washington A. Roebling, the invalid engineer of the bridge, will not witness the ceremonies." That was only partly true. From his rear-window post Colonel Roebling had a good view of the proceedings with his telescope. Emily was too busy to watch. Representing both of them just as she had for years, she and their son, John, were to be part of the ceremony. They were to drive to the Brooklyn side of the bridge in the same victoria Emily had ridden in earlier. There they would greet President Arthur as he and his party crossed the bridge from New York.

After an afternoon of formal speeches in the newly opened Brooklyn terminal building, the President was invited to a reception in the Roebling home. If Colonel Roebling wasn't able to go to the President, Emily had decided, then the President would come to him. And their house would be properly decorated for the occasion. Flowers filled every room. Flags, shields, flowers and banners covered the whole front of the house. A band would play. New busts of John A. and Colonel Roebling would be on display. It would be a party fit for a President. Or the builder of the Brooklyn Bridge.

Now the streets on both sides of the East River were packed with spectators. The *New York Times* wrote, "For blocks and blocks on either side of the bridge there was scarcely a foot of room to spare. The piers were black with people." Flags and decorations and Chinese lanterns hung from every building. Rooftops and windows were jammed. All kinds of boats crowded the river, their flags and streamers a fluttering patchwork of color. The six warships of the North Atlantic Squadron were already in position in the East River. And then it was almost two o'clock, and the ceremony began. Led by the Seventh Regiment and its seventy-five-piece band, President Arthur, his cabinet and the rest of his party stepped smartly out on the elevated promenade from the New York side and started across the bridge.

With the band playing "Hail to the Chief," the board of trustees of the New York Bridge Company greeted the President at the New York anchorage, then joined him for the rest of his walk across the bridge. When the party reached the New York tower, the Fifth U.S. Artillery joined the procession. As they marched between lines of uniformed troops, the fleet of warships fired a salute. So did cannons at the U.S. Navy Yard, Fort Greene and other forts in the harbor. Factory whistles screeched, steam whistles blew, bells rang and the Trinity Church bells chimed. The seven thousand invited guests on the roadway deck beneath the elevated promenade cheered and applauded. The Regiment band played "Hail to the Chief" at least six more times.

And then the President reached the Brooklyn side. Emily Roebling, the mayor of Brooklyn, the Twenty-third Regiment and its band were there to

President Chester A. Arthur leads the procession across the elevated promenade during Opening Day ceremonies, May 24, 1883.

greet him officially. The President's walk was over, and though it was only a short walk, in a real sense it was a long hero's journey. And the hero was Colonel Roebling. Even the cheering crowds were aware that the brief crossing symbolized the triumph of an amazing human spirit.

But the crowds were cheering for more than an individual. They were cheering for the bridge itself. It didn't matter now that the bridge had taken two and one half times as long as the five years John Roebling had predicted or had cost $15,500,000, more than twice the original estimate. Expressing both energy and movement, the bridge was considered the greatest engineering feat of the century. It was, in fact, called the Eighth Wonder of the World. The Brooklyn Bridge marked a new era, and bridge building would never be the same again. With a newfound willingness to try the untried, bridges that had once been considered impossible were suddenly brought within the range of the imagination.

Longer suspension bridges would be built in the future, but they would basically only be extensions of what the pioneering Roeblings had invented and developed. Every step of the building of the Brooklyn Bridge had been a breakthrough—the sinking of enormous underwater caissons as foundations for the towers, the unique design of the anchorages, the spinning of parallel cable wires great distances in the air, the galvanizing of all wires and wire ropes, the extensive system of trusses that made the superstructure rigid.

But above all, and for the first time, the Brooklyn Bridge utilized both the structural and artistic possibilities of steel. It was the beginning of a heroic new age, the age of skyscrapers. By 1883 New York was beginning to run out of space. Now, with the Brooklyn Bridge demonstrating the successful use of steel, architects began to think in terms of high-rise construction, and essential to this development was the use of steel cables for elevators.

As for the artistic possibilities of steel, the beauty of the Brooklyn Bridge was obvious. Its airy spiderweb of steel suspenders and stays and the graceful curve of its great cables contrasted with the solidity of its mammoth granite towers. As a magazine article declared at the time, "The bridge is beautiful in itself."

But more than an engineering feat and more than its physical beauty, the Brooklyn Bridge had become a uniting force. It had, as promised, not only mastered nature, but it also represented in a profound and visual way all that was best in America in 1883. America could accomplish anything when there was that kind of hope for the future and when there was that desire to dream and plan beyond known horizons.

To the immigrants arriving by the thousands in nearby Castle Garden, it was immediate, visual proof of what an immigrant could achieve, for it was well known that an immigrant had designed the bridge and that mostly immigrant labor had built it. Because the bridge was a part of and yet detached from the city, it provided an escape from crowded city living. It was a vantage point from which to see the nearby streets, the skyline, distant vistas and even oneself from a new perspective. A writer of the day suggested, "But the wise man will not cross the bridge in five minutes nor in twenty. He will linger to get the good of the splendid sweep of view about him . . ." From the start the bridge had its place as a living part of the American heritage.

After the President's walk a thousand guests, including governors and representatives from almost all thirty-eight states, senators, members of Congress, army and navy officers, bridge employees and the press, listened to what must have seemed like an endless afternoon of speeches, taking nearly three hours in all. Of all the words spoken, perhaps Brooklyn mayor Seth Low's summed up best how people felt about the bridge. "No one who has been upon it can ever forget it."

The Roeblings weren't forgotten, either. The president of the board of trustees of the New York Bridge Company said, "With one name, in an especial sense, this Bridge will always be associated—that of Roebling."

At last the speeches were over and it was on to the Roeblings' reception. The President, the governor, the mayors of both Brooklyn and New York and hundreds of other guests were greeted by both Roeblings in their front parlor. The President visited for an hour, and Colonel Roebling stayed downstairs the whole time. But as soon as the President left, Colonel Roebling left, too. As he slowly climbed back up the stairs, the guests burst into applause. It was the only public tribute Colonel Roebling had received for almost fourteen years' service as chief engineer of the bridge.

One hundred and fifty thousand people crossed the bridge during that afternoon and evening. In fact, it took an hour and a half to clear the bridge at dusk, when the newly installed electric lights were turned on. Seventy arc lamps blazed overhead in a curving light that stretched from Brooklyn to New York. Although probably few people realized it at the time, the all-steel bridge lit by electricity was a dramatic forecast of the doors that the Roeblings had opened for the builders of the future.

At eight o'clock a solitary rocket sailed into the air from the bridge. It was a signal. The bridge lights flicked off.

Crash! Boom!

Fifty rockets exploded high over the river span of the bridge, while twenty bombs soared up from the towers. For the next hour 14 tons of fireworks blazed from the bridge and the tops of the two towers. At each burst a huge roar went up from the crowds, which now numbered in the hundreds of thousands. It was a celebration like no other celebration New York had ever seen. Rockets were going off up and down the river and all over both cities. Every boat joined in the clamor with bells, whistles, band music and rockets of their own.

At nine o'clock, in a spectacular finale, five hundred rockets were fired at once. They hung suspended over the river like enormous floodlights, dazzling the whole skyline. Every whistle, horn, bell and noisemaker joined in. People yelled themselves hoarse, and bands played through the night.

What were Colonel Roebling and Emily thinking as they watched from their upstairs room, where they had watched the bridge for so many years? Neither of them ever said, but they must have felt pride and triumph mingled with a certain sadness and regret.

Fireworks display on Opening Day. *(overleaf)*

E·P·I·L·O·G·U·E

THE BROOKLYN BRIDGE still stands and to this day is the most photographed, painted, written about and perhaps best loved man-made structure in America. Certainly it is America's, if not the world's, most famous bridge. In 1944 engineers went over the bridge inch by inch to determine what structural changes were needed. Although they already knew the Roeblings had designed and built the bridge six times stronger than had been necessary at the time, they were concerned about the ever-increasing weight of traffic. The study took two years. Their conclusion? The bridge needed a coat of paint.

Since then the roadways have been widened, the trolley and L-tracks removed and extra trusswork added, although none of the changes altered the basic structure or appearance of the bridge. Recently, however, the diagonal steel stays and suspenders have shown the corroding effects of air pollution, of the heavy use of salt and chemicals for snow removal and of acids from pigeon droppings. Extensive repair work is planned on the stays and suspenders. But structurally? The Brooklyn Bridge is as sound today as it was when it opened on that lovely May day in 1883.

As for Colonel Roebling, soon after the bridge was finished his eyesight began to improve so that he could once again read and write and even go outside. A year later he and Emily moved to Troy, New York, to be near their son, who was a student at Rensselaer Polytechnic Institute, as Colonel Roebling and Colonel Roebling's four brothers had been before him. After four years in Troy the Roeblings moved to Trenton, New Jersey, near the family wire rope factory.

Gradually Colonel Roebling's health improved. It was as if during his years in Brooklyn he had needed all his physical strength simply to wage his battle with the bridge. Once the battle was won, he could focus his energies on regaining his health. Although he wrote to his son in 1911, "I have been fighting this trouble of mine for 40 years," Colonel Roebling outlived every major figure connected with the bridge. After running the family wire rope business for five years in the 1920s, he died in 1926 at the age of eighty-nine.

Total length of bridge   5989 feet

Length of river span   1595½ feet

Length of each land span   930 feet

Length of Brooklyn approach   971 feet

Length of New York approach   1562½ feet

Height of bridge in center of river span   135 feet

Launching size and weight of Brooklyn caisson   168 feet x 102 feet x 14½ feet;
3000 tons

Launching size and weight of New York caisson   172 feet x 102 feet x 14½ feet;
3250 tons

Depth of Brooklyn caisson below high water   44½ feet

Depth of New York caisson below high water   78½ feet

Height of towers above high water   276½ feet

Height of towers above roadway   159 feet

Height of tower arches above roadway   117 feet

Width of arches   33¾ feet

Size of each anchorage at base   129 feet x 119 feet

Size of each anchorage at top   117 feet x 104 feet

Height of each anchorage in front   89 feet

Height of each anchorage in rear   85 feet

Weight of each anchorage   60,000 tons

Number of anchor plates in each anchorage   4

Size and weight of each anchor plate   16 feet x 17½ feet x 2½ feet; 23 tons

Number of anchor bars in each anchorage   872

Number of cables   4

Number of strands in each cable   19

Total length of wire in each cable   approximately 3600 miles

Diameter of each cable   15¾ inches

Miles of wrapping wire on each cable   243 miles 943 feet

Strength of each cable   11,200 tons

Number of suspenders   1520

Number of diagonal stays   400

Width of bridge floor   85 feet

Width of elevated promenade   15 feet 7 inches

Height of promenade above roadway   11½ feet

Grade of roadway   3¼ feet in 100 feet

Total weight of bridge, not including caissons, towers, anchorages   14,680 tons

· BIBLIOGRAPHY ·

Barnes, Alfred Cutler. *The New York and Brooklyn Bridge*. Brooklyn: Copyright by J. H. Fisher, 1883.

Conant, William C. "The Brooklyn Bridge," *Harper's New Monthly Magazine* (May, 1883): 923–46.

Condit, Carl. *American Building Art: the nineteenth century*. New York: Oxford University Press, 1960.

Construction Industry Standards and Interpretations. U.S. Department of Labor Occupational Safety and Health Administration, vol. 3. Washington, D.C.: 1980.

Crane, Hart. *The Bridge*. New York: Liveright Publishing Corporation, 1933.

Farrington, Edmond F. *History of the Building of the Great Bridge*. New York: Mooney & Co., 27 Chambers Street, 1881.

First Annual Reports of the Chief Engineer and General Superintendent of the East River Bridge, June 12, 1870. Brooklyn: Eagle Book and Job Printing Department, 1870.

Gies, Joseph. *Bridges and Men*. Garden City, New York: Doubleday & Company, 1963.

Grafton, John. *New York in the 19th Century, Engravings from "Harper's Weekly" and other Contemporary Sources*. New York: Dover Publications, 1977.

Green, S. W. *A Complete History of the New York and Brooklyn Bridge from its Conception in 1866 to its Completion in 1883*. New York: S. W. Green's Son, 1883.

Harper's Weekly, vol. 14 (November 19, 1870): 738, 744.

Harper's Weekly, vol. 14 (December 17, 1870): 812.

Harper's Weekly, vol. 27 (May 26, 1883): 325–26.

Hyman, Stanley Edgar. "This Alluring Roadway." *New Yorker* (May 17, 1952): 39–84.

John A. Roebling. An Account at the Unveiling of a Monument to His Memory. Trenton: Roebling Press, 1908.

John A. Roebling's Sons Company. *Suspension Bridges.* Trenton, N.J.: 1931.

Kouwenhoven, John A. *Columbia Historical Portrait of New York.* Garden City, N.Y.: Doubleday and Company, 1953.

McCullough, David. *The Great Bridge.* New York: Simon and Schuster, 1972.

Morrison, John H. *History of American Steam Navigation.* New York: Stephen Daye Press, 1958.

Mumford, John K. *Outspinning the Spider.* New York: Robert L. Stillson Company, 1921.

Mumford, Lewis. *Roots of Contemporary Architecture.* New York: Grove Press, 1952.

———— *Sticks and Stones.* New York: Horace Liveright, 1924.

Opening Ceremonies of the New York and Brooklyn Bridge. Brooklyn: Eagle Print, 1883.

Perry, John. *American Ferryboats.* New York: Wilfred Funk, 1957.

Report of the Board of Consulting Engineers to the Directors of the New York Bridge Company. Brooklyn: Standard Press, 1869.

Report of the Chief Engineer and General Superintendent to the Board of Directors of the New York Bridge Company, June 5, 1871. Brooklyn: Eagle Book and Job Printing Department, 1871.

Report of the Chief Engineer and Superintendent of the New York and Brooklyn Bridge, June 1, 1884. Brooklyn: Eagle Book and Job Printing Department, 1884.

Report of the Chief Engineer of the New York and Brooklyn Bridge, January 1, 1877. Brooklyn: Eagle Print, 1877.

Report of the General Superintendent to Hon. Henry C. Murphy, President of the New York Bridge Company. Submitted by William C. Kingsley, General Superintendent.

Report of John A. Roebling, Chief Engineer, to the President and Directors of the New York Bridge Company of the Proposed East River Bridge. Brooklyn: Daily Eagle Print, 1867.

Report of John A. Roebling, Chief Engineer, to the President and Directors of the New York Bridge Company, on the Proposed East River Bridge. Brooklyn: Eagle Book and Job Printing Department, 1870.

Reports of the Executive Committee, Chief Engineer, and General Superintendent, of the New York Bridge Company, June 1, 1872. Brooklyn: Eagle Book and Job Printing Department, 1872.

Roebling, Washington A. *Life of John A. Roebling, Chief Engineer, By his oldest son Washington A. Roebling.* Rutgers University Archibald S. Alexander Library, Special Collections.

Schuyler, Hamilton. *The Roeblings, A Century of Engineers, Bridgebuilders and Industrialists*. Princeton, N.J.: Princeton University Press, 1931.

Scientific American. (September 22, 1883): 176ff.

Shirley-Smith, H. *The World's Great Bridges*. New York: Harper & Row, 1965.

Smith, Andrew H., M.D. *The Effects of High Atmospheric Pressure Including Caisson Disease*. Brooklyn: Eagle Book and Job Printing Department, 1873.

Steinman, David B. *Builders of the Bridge*. New York: Harcourt, Brace and Company, 1945.

Steinman, David B., and Watson, Sara Ruth. *Bridges and Their Builders*. New York: G. P. Putnam's Sons, 1941.

"To-day's Great Ceremony." *The New York Times*, vol 32 (May 24, 1883): 1–2.

Trachtenberg, Alan. *Brooklyn Bridge, Fact and Symbol*. New York: Oxford University Press, 1965.

"Two Great Cities United." *The New York Times*, vol. 32 (May 25, 1883): 1–2.

Van Dyke, John C. *The New New York*. New York: The Macmillan Company, 1909.

White, Norval, and Willensky, Elliot, editors. *AIA Guide to New York City*. New York: The Macmillan Company, 1967.

· INDEX ·

Page numbers in italics refer to photographs.